Seven Years of Apparitions

Fall, 1988

THE RIEHLE FOUNDATION

Front cover photos: Maria during an apparition. Back cover photos: Ivanka with
Fr. Laurentin and her daughter Christina.

Seven Years of Apparitions

Time for the Harvest?
Latest News From Medjugorje Number 7
Fall, 1988

by
René Laurentin

Edited and Published by
THE RIEHLE FOUNDATION
P.O. Box 7
Milford, Ohio 45150

The publisher recognizes and accepts that the final authority regarding the apparitions at Medjugorje rests with the Holy See of Rome, to whose judgment we willingly submit.

—The Publisher

Published by The Riehle Foundation
For additional copies, write:
The Riehle Foundation
P.O. Box 7
Milford, Ohio 45150

This book originally published as *"7 Annees D'Apparitions,"* June, 1988 by O.E.I.L., Paris, France.

Copyright © 1988 The Riehle Foundation

Library of Congress Catalog Card No.: 88-063312

ISBN: 0-9618840-7-X

Interior photos by: Fr. Jack Wintz, O.F.M.
                        St. Anthony Messenger
                        Cincinnati, Ohio

St. James Church—Medjugorje

TABLE OF CONTENTS

APPENDIX AND DOCUMENTS

SEPARATE ARTICLES

FOREWORD

This seventh edition of The Latest News covers a year of apparitions in Medjugorje: from the celebration of the sixth anniversary (24-25 of June 1987), to the threshold of the seventh anniversary: June, 1988.

This period seems at present the clearest and most significant, until the revelations of the secrets and the end of the apparitions.

It is also the period of the beginning of attacks through the print media, all aimed at discrediting the individuals involved in Medjugorje. Such attacks never seem to concern themselves with the fruits realized during this seven year period.

Chapter 1

SIXTH ANNIVERSARY
OF THE APPARITIONS IN MEDJUGORJE

(June 24-25, 1987)

Thursday, June 25, 1987, the crowd in Medjugorje surpassed all records for the sixth anniversary of the apparitions. I was there for my 15th trip.

The parish church loomed like a ship rising from the ocean; the crowd was larger, and more prayerful than ever. It was overflowing on all sides—on the road congested with buses and cars, in the fields and in the yard of the rectory.

Approximately 150 priests, (some of them having heard confessions for as long as 10 to 12 hours) were scattered in this crowd, both inside and outside of the church. More than 100 priests distributed Holy Communion at the liturgy, which took a long time. In my judgment, there were more people than last year. The Marxist newspapers (now benevolent), generously estimated this crowd at 400,000 people. I would say over 100,000. But this minimum figure is perhaps below the actual number. Everyone knew well that Cardinal Kuharic, president of the Episcopal Conference (and the person primarily responsible for the judgment on the apparitions) specifically stated that one can come here to pray in all good conscience, and fruitfully.

JUNE 24, VIGIL OF THE ANNIVERSARY

On June 24, 1987 (6th anniversary of the day when the apparition first appeared near the top of the hill), after the customary ceremonies, Maria invited the pilgrims to climb Mt. Krizevac, in anticipation of a second apparition at 11:30 that night. Thousands of people scaled the 540 meters of the mountain, in uninterrupted lines on the small path, and recited the Rosary. Later, the apparition appeared. Afterward, Maria stated:

"The Virgin was happy. First of all she prayed over all of us. We asked her to bless us, which she did. Then she gave us in substance this message":

1

> *Dear children, I wish to lead you on the road to conversion. Convert the world, I desire it. Let your life be conversion for others. Do not fall into infidelity. May each one of you abandon yourself to my will and the will of God. I give you special graces, and especially the gift of conversion. May each one of you carry it with you. My blessing truly incites one to conversion.*

"Then she prayed again, for a moment, over all of us. We (the seers) prayed to her for all your needs, for each one of you present here. Finally the Virgin said: *Go in the peace of God.* Then she left" (Ode).

For the Blessed Virgin, this exceptional visit was not that of the anniversary, but of its vigil. As a matter of fact, for her, as she has stressed to the seers for several years, the 24th of June 1981 is not the day of the first apparition but a prelude, because the group of six seers had not yet been formed. Only four of them had been there for that first contact, from a distance and in fear, without daring even to climb the hill, but which they did the following day, June 25. It is on that day that they saw her up close and began to converse with her. It is that day, June 25, that is the anniversary.

JUNE 25, 1987

On June 25, 1987, five seers had the apparition in Medjugorje, something that had not happened for three years. And these apparitions took place in three different places.

After an exhausting day, Vicka had her apparition at home, as usual for reasons of health. Her house had been besieged since early that morning, to the point that cars which were arriving were not able to pass on the narrow street in front of her door. The crowd reached the limits of incomprehensibility, but in an astonishing calm. Vicka then emerged, smiling, friendly, modest, a transparent witness of She who surpasses her.

Three seers (Maria, Ivan and Jakov) had the apparition at the rectory. It is from there that Maria had been receiving the messages on the 25th of each month. These teaching messages do not aim to simply repeat, but to cause the internalization of the unappreciated gift of God. The message of that day was:

> *Dear children, I thank all of you today, and invite you to the peace of God. Let each one of you in his heart attain the peace which God gives you. I bless all of you today with a blessing which comes from God. Dear children, follow in life, my path. I beseech you, I love you, dear children. That is why I have renewed my calls, I do not know how many times. I thank you for everything which you have done according to my intentions. Help me, I beg you, so that I may be able to offer to God to save you and to guide you on the road to salvation. Thank you for responding to my call.*

Ivanka had her annual apparition, the second one since May 7, 1985 when daily apparitions ceased for her. The Gospa had promised her a yearly apparition, beginning 1986: . . .*the anniversary day of the first apparition, June 25.* (Since 1983, Mirjana also has an annual apparition on her birthday, which is March 18). Ivanka's second extraordinary apparition took place at the house of her brother-in-law who had just built a guest house near the front of the church on land which his wife had inherited. I was there and I transcribed my notes which I had been taking progressively:

> I arrived at the hour which had been set for me, 15 minutes till 6:00, with Darla Klanac, a Croatian residing in Canada. I was the first one there. Then there quickly followed the grandmother, the father, some members of the family, and some Italian friends, notably Jacopini and Pallavicini, excellent photographers. And then Ivanka arrived—happy, light-hearted, harmonious. She's expecting a baby the middle of November and she is already in her

fourth month. That doesn't change her slender sil-
houette. Her grandmother extends her arms to her,
and there is a prolonged affectionate exchange between them, which renews a friendship from the
difficult years since after the death of her mother
(April 1981). Ivanka helped her grandmother with
her housecleaning, something that demanded a great
deal of suppleness on her part. For nearly a year,
she resided at the home of her in-laws where this
collaboration continued, in an ideal cooperation with
her mother-in-law. It is now 6:15. Ivanka asks Darla
Klanac to begin the Rosary: the Joyful Mysteries,
in Croatian. She herself kneels four or five meters
in front of the wall toward the back of the room,
facing the icons of Christ and the Blessed Virgin
which have been arranged for the occasion. The
prayer is solid and fervent, in the customary style
of Medjugorje. My vocational bias (critical) acts
in spite of everything. I ask myself "will she see?"
She has not seen her for a year and so many things
have changed for her. Here she is married, very
soon the mother of a family. Yesterday she returned
from her first trip abroad: Italy, Scotland, France
(Nice and Lourdes). I wonder if her receptiveness
has not changed? But Ivanka seemed calm and without apprehension, a little tired perhaps because of
her pregnancy. But no sign of anxiety.

She knelt down seated on her heels. Toward the
end of the first Rosary she straightens up, always
on her knees. A mother, a close relative, comes
to place on the floor almost in front of her, a baby,
which she had had in her arms, and which is play-
ing graciously with his hands. Ivanka glances at this
child, a reminder of the child for whom she is
waiting.

Toward 6:30, the recitation of the Rosary passes
on to the Italians; the Sorrowful Mysteries are said
in their language. At 6:44, Ivanka advances a few

steps toward the little table which has been set before the wall. She recites the "Our Father," just as she had always done before in her daily apparitions. And suddenly, she kneels down with that briskness which made her generally more prompt than the others. Her voice disappears, and her countenance reflects the limpid joy of her meeting. Conversation and contemplation alternate. At the end of two minutes (6:47), her voice reappears to pray with the Blessed Virgin, who had started the "Our Father" followed by the "Glory Be." Then Ivanka's voice disappears again. The conversation is taken up inaudibly. Contemplation is prolonged. At 6:53, this conversation takes a lively turn. Ivanka's smile became mischievous and tender at the same time, as if the Virgin's remark amused her. She had found the familiarity of the past.

At 6:55 her glance is raised (as always at the end of the apparitions as the Virgin disappears, while ascending). Ivanka murmurs: "Ode" (Gone!), an exclamation with which the seers often emphasize the end of the apparition. She gets up. It is over until next year. Very simply, she turns toward those who have prayed with her.

"The Gospa spoke to me especially about the first and the second secrets. She asks you to pray very much with regard to them." she says. This mention of the first two secrets (which are also the first two "warnings") does not mean that their revelation is near. Would this pressing invitation to pray mean that these warnings concern the grave threats which sin has waged on the world? I do not know because the third secret (which is also the third "warning," the visible sign to be given on the hill in order to convince those who do not yet believe) has an evidently positive character. It was not advisable to ask Ivanka more about it. Nevertheless, I dared to ask a question (professional conscience of the informant): "What made you smile in such a tender and amusing way before the end of the apparition?" She simply smiled, and in a very strange way, that concerned me.

When our Lady will come on the 25th of June 1988, Ivanka will undoubtedly be accompanied by her baby. (Which will then be nine months old, since I know, as of this writing, that this baby was born on November 11, 1987, and her name is Christina, a model baby.) Ivanka has assured me that she will take her with her for the apparition.

Chapter 2

A BOMB AMID THE PEACE

Feast day of St. James

The 25th of July 1987, day of Saint James, is a feast day at Medjugorje; made more special every three years by the coming of the bishop for Confirmation. This was the case in 1987, six years after the well-known Confirmation of July 25, 1981, when the bishop declared forcefully:

"I am profoundly convinced that no one has influenced these young people, who affirm to have seen the Gospa. I affirm, and I guarantee that no priest has tried to influence them. They say exactly what is in their hearts. I am sure that these young people are not lying! No, they are not lying!"

This day, July 25, 1987, the crowd was overflowing the church. The ceremony began with fervor for the many young people, visibly well prepared for their Confirmation in this fervent parish, which holds the records for quantity and quality, for Confirmation as well as for everything else.

A SHOCKING SERMON

And here it is that Monsignor Zanic began to speak. It was not to speak of the Holy Spirit, nor of Confirmation, nor of the apostle Saint James, but of the apparitions, which was the cause of this crowd and this fervor.

It was an indictment filled with emotion, which separated the tree from its good fruits:

> "One prays here and fasts very much. But all that is done in the conviction that the events, which have taken place here, are really supernatural. Well, for those who preach to the people and the faithful things which are not true on the subject of God, Jesus Christ, the Blessed Virgin Mary, they deserve the bottom of Hell."

His shocking comments were rude and ungracious, because it tended to disassociate the fervent parishioners from the clergy, who he claimed were guilty of cultivating these apparitions and thus bent for damnation. The bishop did not forget that a new inquiry commission was formed by Cardinal Kuharic to study these problems, but he found there another reason for condemning it.

> "Some (and the priests of the parish are always the target) have been precipitous (. . .). They have anticipated the judgment of the Church. They have proclaimed that there were miracles and supernatural events. They preached these private revelations from the altar, something which is never permitted as long as the Church has not recognized such revelations as authentic."

Here the bishop recalled his thesis of 1984, which tended to forbid the pilgrimages. The Episcopal Conference, concerned with the respect of Canon law and the inalienable Christian freedoms, had stated, through Bishop Franic, president of the doctrinal and liturgical commission, that by "official pilgrimage" one means those which are authorized by a bishop. Monsignor Zanic enlarged and extended this circle of forbidden pilgrimages to include all pilgrimages formed by the faithful which "officially" arrive and leave together.

Monsignor Zanic founded his indictment on the work of his own Commission, which Rome had asked him to dissolve on May 2, 1986, before its term.

> —"This work has produced the following results," he proclaimed:
> —"Two members of the Commission have expressed a favorable vote;
> —One of them has abstained;
> —Another has declared that 'perhaps at the beginning there is something,' then. . .?
> —The other 11 voted against; non constat de supernaturalitate, that is to say: there were no apparitions."[1]

But the bishop tried to make people forget (appendix page 92) that Rome had dissolved this commission before it could accomplish its work. The answers hastily gathered before the dissolution had a rather relative value. "A response would be premature," said some of the members. And, when the bishop maintained his request for a vote of orientation, they asked that it be done under the seal of secrecy. It seemed to them that they had obtained this assurance but it was not respected, because the bishop divulged the vote to his visitors, shortly thereafter.

But particularly, the bishop did not recall the objective of the question asked: "Constat de supernaturalitate?" (Is the supernatural character evident?) Only two members had answered yes. But in an unfinished stage of the investigation, it would be imprudent to categorically affirm evidence of the supernatural, which only two members did in a strong manner. Thus the majority of the answers were dubious or negative. Monsignor Zanic interpreted this prudence, as an absolute disqualification of the apparitions:

"The supernatural character is not evident," the majority of the members of the commission had answered.

"The non-supernatural character of the events is evident," the bishop had them say. The question asked should have been: "Ultrum constat de non supernaturalitate?" (Has the non-supernatural character of the apparition been established?)

He stressed in continuing his sermon:

> "All the members of the commission have worked conscientiously; they have examined everything which could serve to discover the truth."

That was much to say, since the 300 sick who had been declared cured, were not particularly examined or interviewed, and the most independent members of the commission complained of a lack of documentation, and restrictions imposed on the inquiry.

The bishop pursued:

"The Church cannot put its credibility into play. She has often maintained a distance from the large crowds, who have assembled at places where it had been established that the events were not of a supernatural origin."

And here the bishop cited the apparitions at Garabandal and at San Damiano. Then, he spoke, ironically, about the diversity of successive places, where the apparitions of Medjugorje have taken place:

"At Podbrdo, on the hill Crnica, in the homes, in the gardens, in the fields, in the vineyards, in the tobacco plantations, in the church, on the altar, in the sacristy, in the choir loft, on the street, on the road to Cerno, in a car, on a bus, at school, at certain places of Mostar, at Sarajevo, in the convents, at Zagreb, at Varazdin, in Switzerland, in Italy, on Mount Krizevac, in the parish, at the rectory, etc. Certainly, this list does not comprise even half the places of the alleged apparitions."

As humorous and incongruent as this potpourri may seem, the bishop did not invent anything. It is true that the places of the apparitions had been very diverse. But that was due simply to the fact that the Blessed Virgin appeared to the children at a certain hour, wherever they were, and that changed very often, in part due to the prohibition by the police, but also by that of the bishop. While he considered this preciseness, Monsignor Zanic concluded cheerfully:

"Every serious person who venerates Our Lady must then ask himself: Oh Blessed Virgin, what have they done with you? The apparitions deviate the spirit, they are the source of controversy," he continued. And he announced, consequently, some disciplinary measures:

"All those priests who organize pilgrimages, and

> who come here attributing a supernatural character
> to these events, I forbid them to celebrate Mass in
> my diocese, as long as the Episcopal Conference
> has not concluded its work."

Did Monsignor Zanic forbid the celebration of Mass within his diocese, to priests who were organizing pilgrimages (there were practically none, since the priests left the organization of these un-official pilgrimages to lay people), or, more broadly, to those who attributed a supernatural character to the events? I asked myself: how does one interpret these words from the bishop? Would those who had been forbidden to celebrate, really bear the pain of suspension? I asked Cardinal Ratzinger, then Cardinal Kuharic the same question. The latter advised me to write about it to the bishop, since he did not want to answer in his place. I then wrote to Monsignor Zanic, telling him that except for a contrary warning on his part, I did not think that he intended to forbid me from celebrating Mass during my stays in his diocese, because I did not organize any pilgrimages, and also, that I would subordinate and submit my reasons as an expert, to the final judgment of the Church. Finally, that my personal conviction remained open to every fact or objective correction, and to every legitimate order of authority. Monsignor Zanic, sometimes over zealous in his interventions, but wise and moderate in his daily administration, and respectful of canon law, did not contest my interpretation.

He finished his sermon as he had begun it, invoking the Blessed Virgin:

> "I, your servant, Bishop of Mostar, before all of
> these people who call upon you, I recognize and
> accept your great sign."

That created some suspense. Was he going to finish by accepting that the sign predicted by the seers could settle the question in favor of the apparitions? Previously, he had said several times: "If the great sign which has been announced is convincing, I will be the first to recognize it!" No, "the sign" on which he concluded his sermon was the Partheon shot:—a kind of boomerang, which came back in decisive objection to the sign announced by the seers.

"I do not personally need a sign. But a sign is necessary for those who believe, and believe what is false. The sign consists in the fact that after six years you (the Gospa) always remained silent, in spite of the repeated announcement that you where going to give a sign. The seers already said in 1981:

'There will be a visible and lasting sign on the hill of the apparitions. It is going to come, one will see it in a short time, wait a little more. A little patience.' And still again:

'The sign will take place in 1981, for the feast of the Immaculate Conception, for Christmas, or for New Year's Day, etc.'[2]

I thank you, O Our Lady, for having responded sufficiently by your silence of six years. Intervene especially in favor of this land and this parish where, an infinity of times, one has used your holy name to spread the messages which were not from you. Dain to cause them to cease inventing such messages which have been presented as coming from you. O very Blessed Virgin, dain finally to accept in reparation, the sincere prayers of pious souls who remain at a distance, from the fanaticism and the disobedience toward the Church."

THE RISK

While defying the opinion of a fervent and unanimous people, the bishop summoned great courage: "I risk my life in opposition to the fanatics of the apparitions," he often repeated to his visitors.

To openly confront this parish, which he accused of fanaticism, was, in his own perspective, the limit of temerity, because Monsignor Zanic (a Croatian himself), knew from

experience how the Croats were incandescent. He had had
a rude experience in other places and circumstances. Before
the apparitions, while he was founding the Cathedral at Mostar,
in order to transfer the parishes from the old Franciscan
churches of his Episcopal city, the parishioners reacted ruth-
lessly. When the Bishop of Mostar sent a secular priest to
Grude, instead of a Franciscan, the parishioners locked the
church until he, who was regarded as an intruder, left.

At Medjugorje, the shock was certainly more terrible and
more vital than at Mostar or at Grude, because the words
of the bishop changed not only their habits, it pierced through
their hearts. Monsignor Zanic knew well what he was doing.
He waited for a manifestation, some stormy uprising that would
permit him to publish to the whole world that Medjugorje
was a parish in revolt, without respect for the bishop; that
there were the fruits of these false apparitions.

PRAYER AND RESPECT

But this parish was formed by trials during these years. Some
even went to prison in support of the apparitions. They learned
to accept everything in peace, while subduing the reactive vigor
of their temperament. From one extreme of the bishop's sermon to the other, not a word, not a gesture, not a protest.

"What did you think during the sermon?" I asked one of
the parishioners from Bijakovici, the hamlet of the seers.

"We prayed for the bishop," he answered me.

The respect for the successor of the apostles was stronger
than the affliction. Once again, the parish and the hearts were
governed by the message of Our Lady: "Reconciliation."

Monsignor Zanic, always ready to draw from each fact a conclusion favorable to his struggle, saw in this heroic patience,
a new sign of his success. He interprets it as an approval of his
opposition, and silent hostility to the apparitions themselves:

"You see well," says he on his departure, "they did
not react. They are tired of these apparitions. My sermon has freed them. Their silence gives proof of it."

The priests gave proof by the same respectful and conciliatory silence. After the ceremony, according to custom, these priests, whom he had publicly condemned "to the bottom of Hell," received the bishop for the meal of the patron's feast. However, on his arrival at the rectory, the youngest of them, Father Petar, very spontaneously expressed to him, in private, his astonishment over so many attacks and incoherences. Father Ivan Dugandzic, spiritual director of the parish, after reflection, later wrote an open letter in order to clear the ambiguities, which the publication of the sermon had enormously spread in the world press (appendix page 100).

AN EFFECTIVE OPERATION IN THE WORLD PRESS

In effect, given the good reception to his provoking indictment, Monsignor Zanic had translations made of it, notably in Italian and in English, and had them widely published. These publications began in Italy, where he personally went during the month of August, 1987, to contact the journal with the widest circulation in the peninsula (2 million readers), "Famiglia Christiana," (Christian Families—Sept. 2, 1987), and other Catholic weeklies. The article and second hand dispatches, often simplified the question by stating that "the bishop of the place, responsible for the matter, condemned the apparitions," (while forgetting that Rome had removed him from this judgment in May 1986).

For the third time, news circulated in the world that the bishop responsible had given a negative judgment, forbidden the pilgrimages, and taken sanctions against whomever exceeded this order. And many of the faithful, who owed their deep conversion to Medjugorje, received orders or instructions from their priests not to go there anymore, in the name of obedience to the Church. It presented trouble for their consciences, because some asked themselves:

"Should we not believe anymore? If what faith has given us is false, according to the Church herself, what then is our faith worth?"

We find here again, the same old story, spreading false news. We, and others have covered it before in previous books. The causes are always the same: the adversaries of Medjugorje (the press and religious), endorse by magnifying the opposition of Monsignor Zanic to the apparitions. Of course, he is still the Bishop of Mostar. In this regard, he deserves the respect and obedience which the parish of Medjugorje is first to manifest to him. But, since Rome removed him from the judgment, it is no longer correct that he declare himself as the "responsible bishop."

THE DEBATE AMONG THE CROATIAN BISHOPS (September 16, 1987)

The results of this intervention concerned the Episcopal Conference, to whom Rome had transferred judgment over this matter, on a national and even international basis. Cardinal Kuharic, president of the Conference, then convened in an extraordinary meeting, the Croatian Bishops at Zagreb, on September 16, 1987, to clarify the confusion born from this surprising intervention. Its principal problems or paradoxes were the following:

1. The bishop, who had been relieved from the judgment, made a public judgment and disseminated it throughout the world.
2. He based it on the (incomplete) work of his Commission, which had been dissolved on orders from Rome.
3. He anticipated the conclusions of the competent Commission named by the cardinal, and whose work was being done with the greatest discretion.
4. He acted contrary to instructions of silence, given by the Yugoslavian Bishops for the duration of their work.
5. He seemed to forbid the pilgrimages, while the Episcopal Conference had always maintained the legitimacy of private pilgrimages according to Canon law, and the rights of Christian freedom. The sponateous support for a genuine apparition and private pilgrimages (individual or collective) could not be forbidden when an apparition took place, without harm to the truth, the faith and morals. The Christian people have the right to interpret, (under the authorized control of the magisterium).

The Church places great value on the judgment of the faithful and regards it as a criterion of authenticity. December 1858, the same year of the Lourdes apparitions, and four years before the official recognition by Bishop Laurence (1862), Don Bosco spoke with fervor about the apparitions in Lourdes, (Lemoyne, "Biographical Memories of Don Bosco," volume 5).

The Episcopal Conference was all the more impeded because it had only accepted regretfully, under pressure from Rome, taking on responsibility for this judgment. Its unwillingness to become involved in this matter was due to the fact that Medjugorje was a sensitive subject for three reasons:

1. With respect to the Marxist government, which was opposed, in principal, to the apparitions.
2. With respect to the old quarrel between Franciscans and secular clergy, which has torn up so many of the parishes or dioceses of Hercegovina.
3. And with respect to the bishop of the place, whom his colleagues had, up until this time, treated with consideration. With a maximum solidarity of support, as much as possible within the limits of the law, they tolerated his negative positions and his dissuasive action.

"The request of the Episcopal Conference," to which Rome would have yielded, in order to make the judgment of the apparitions pass to its level, is one of those official, pious fictions customary in similar cases according to very old traditions and habits.

Certainly the matter, which had passed from a local level to a national level, demanded to be treated at least at a national level. But it was not the bishops of the country which requested it.

On the other hand, the indictment by Monsignor Zanic created a certain problem in the consciences of millions of pilgrims at an *international* level. It caused a flood of letters and telephone calls addressed to the cardinal and to the other bishops. If this enlightenment, which had led them to God, was only an illusion as the bishop was saying, was it necessary to return to lesser belief or to prior disbelief?

The bishop engaged his authority as successor of the apostles, supremely responsible for the faith at Mostar, in stating forcefully:

> "I am, in this diocese, by divine right, the pastor, the master of the faith, and the judge of questions which concern the faith...I have prayed, I have listened, I have read and seen, etc."

Christian consciences were troubled. It was thus that Cardinal Kuharic convened the extraordinary meeting of the Croatian Bishops on September 16, in order to clarify the issue. Up to that moment, the bishops had solidly supported their colleague from Mostar. Those who were favorable to the apparitions remained silent for the most part (except perhaps Monsignor Franic). The others spoke only with reservations, which one could make of the meaning of Monsignor Zanic, who had been able to give the impression that the Episcopal Conference was solidly unfavorable to the apparitions.

This time, the tone was different. Monsignor Zanic pleaded vigorously for the adoption of the propositions of his sermon of July 25, so well disseminated by the world press. He asked his colleagues to:

> "publish a motion unfavorable to the apparitions,"
> and
> "forbid the pilgrimages in a more radical way."

This time his requests were not followed. The other bishops strongly made him see that his interventions were contrary to the decisions of the Holy See, which had relieved him of responsibility, and also to the normal course of the new inquiry, whose conclusions he anticipated in taking advantage of a jurisdiction which no longer belonged to him. If such was not the case, what was the purpose of the inquiry ordered by Rome, under another jurisdiction?

As for the pilgrimages, all the bishops remembered the

previous deliberations of 1984, when the Episcopal Conference, charged by Monsignor Zanic, had excluded official pilgrimages, but had refused to forbid private pilgrimages, authorized by Canon law, custom, and Christian freedom.

After this discussion, for the first time in an emphatic way, Cardinal Kuharic and the bishops did their utmost to go as far as possible in responding to the requests of Monsignor Zanic, Bishop of Mostar.

1. The bishops agreed to be more specific in a stricter sense (less tolerant), what is understood by "official" pilgrimage. It is, as Monsignor Franic said in 1984, a pilgrimage conducted or led "by the bishop of a place or by the pastor of a parish or other institution." They confirmed that the priests must not, as such, organize pilgrimages which give a certain official character. A private pilgrimage could only be organized by the laity.

   All of this is in accordance to the meaning of promotion by the laity. In the meantime, it was clearly stated that these pilgrimages should not be left abandoned, but "accompanied" by priests necessary for Mass, teaching, confessions, spiritual direction and control, because apparitions are ambiguous phenomenon, and must be guided with vigilance. Too many repressions against the apparitions have the results of delivering the sincere faithful to temptation, or avoidable deviations, indeed to contesting priests, to the detriment of the faith. It is important that the private sector of the faith not be that of arbitrary liberation, but that it be continued in the Church, and that the priestly functions be exercised there.

2. Monsignor Zanic also obtained permission from Cardinal Kuharic to send a letter to priests in his diocese asking them that the messages no longer be read from the altar, but maintain private character. The letter stated:

> The bishops of the region of the Croatian language convened on September 16, 1987, at Zagreb, under the chairmanship of the President of the Episcopal

Conference. . .warned that in the territory subjected
to your jurisdiction (the parish of Medjugorje). . .in
the sermons, the catechesis, both in the press and
the mass media, one not publish the alleged messages from the Madonna, or the alleged answers
of the most Blessed Virgin to questions from the
people. Let the preachers and the catechist proclaim
only the authentic Catholic Doctrine, so as not to
prejudice the work of the commission of the
phenomenon in Medjugorje. (Letter of the bishops
to the parish of Medjugorje, September 17, 1987.
Signed: Kuharic.)

3. In order to take upon himself, to the utmost, the arguments
and legitimate positions of the bishop of the place, the Cardinal also recalled, for those who questioned him, different occasions which gave some assurances that they were finding
objections to the apparitions in the course of their examination.

   At the end of this meeting, Monsignor Franic, president
of the Doctrinal Commission of Yugoslavian Bishops, drafted
a memorandum of the pastoral conclusions in an orderly
manner, and distributed it in his diocese. (See appendix
page 107).

   His memorandum included the following points:

A. The apparitions are under an investigation. They are
   neither recognized nor forbidden, or censored. Therefore, prudence and discretion are in order.
B. In these conditions, "official" pilgrimages would be
   premature and remain forbidden.
C. "Private" pilgrimages are acceptable, and no sanction
   of any kind has been issued, neither by the Episcopal
   Conference, nor even by the bishop of the place. But
   the priests may exercise there, their pastoral role of ad-
   visor, confessor, celebrant, etc.

Cardinal Kuharic, president, who was besieged with questions, stressed these three different points, in his answers.

On the other hand, the Cardinal prevented the sermon of Msgr. Zanic (so widely disseminated in the world press beginning in Italy), from being published in the Croatian press. "Glaz Koncila," the great semi-official Catholic periodical, which depended on his authority, was no longer permitted to publish the sermon of July 25th.

NEW TRANSFER OF THE APPARITIONS

On September 9, 1987, a week after the publication of this sermon of July 25th in "Famiglia Cristiana" (Christian Family), and a week before the meeting of the Croatian bishops, Msgr. Zanic forbid the apparitions from taking place in the rectory, where they had taken refuge, after he had forbidden them from taking place in the discreet "little chapel of the apparitions."

It was a new stage in the series of measures taken by the bishop against the pastoral of the pilgrims. The most harsh had been the letter of March 25th, 1985. Msgr. Zanic had enacted in it, a considerable list of restrictions. He had forbidden, beyond the habitual place of the apparitions, prayers of the seers with the crowd, the venerated statue of the apparition, etc.

The priests had obeyed, but not without difficulty, because the previous transfer of the apparitions to the rectory separated the admirable organic unity, wisely set up by the first pastor of the apparitions, Fr. Jozo Zovko. Shocked to see the people run up the hill and show so little willingness to come to church, he had transferred this fervent crowd from the hill of the apparitions to the church, so that an organic unity was established. Thus one had a beautiful progression: from the Rosary, to the apparitions, and to the Mass—the pinnacle and end of all prayer.

What is one to do in light of the bishop's mandate? Once again, the parish proceeded cautiously, because if the seers had the apparitions in their homes, that would separate the apparitions more than ever from the daily liturgy. That would subject the seers and their families to pressures from the crowd in some exhausting conditions. And that would risk putting them at the mercy of the police, because no worship had been authorized outside of the premises of the church. The seers proceeded cautiously then, in this difficult situation.

"In spite of all that, the bishop cannot forbid the Blessed Virgin from appearing," said Maria thoughtfully.

On Sunday, September 13, 1987, she had an apparition at home. On Monday and Tuesday, concerned about being deprived of Mass and daily Communion, she went very discreetly and took refuge in the (closed) choir loft of the church.

The perplexing discussions had created, without knowing it, this solution of the apparitions in the choir loft. There, in contrast to the rectory where some 30 persons vied for position in the room, they were now able to maintain the strictly private character of the apparition, required by Msgr. Zanic. In the parish itself, other priests advised the seers to have the apparition at home, as was the case with Vicka, for reasons of health. And that was often the case with Jakov. Here still, patience and pastoral perseverance prevailed over the inconveniences, and made progress through the new difficulty, because the apparitions in the rectory conglomerated the crowd at a distance from the church, and thus separated the liturgical assembly. This difficulty was now overcome.

At the end of February, 1988, the rumor spread that the Blessed Virgin had decided that the apparitions will take place each day on the hill. It was false news. It had been decided that only on Monday, a day when there was a second apparition on the hill, for the prayer group late in the evening, after Mass, would the hill be utilized, (the 15th and 22nd of February, notably).

FOOTNOTES

1. Monsignor Zanic counted fifteen votes, for there were fifteen members of the commission. But the two doctors had refused to take part in this vote, since its object, purely theological, did not concern them at all. There were then only 13 votes—those of the theologians. Well before the vote, I had expressed my uneasiness that the members of this commission had been chosen (with four exceptions) from among those theologians who were unfavorable to the apparitions. And Monsignor Zanic had issued a critique on this judgment which I was eager to publish (DN 4, p. 81-82). In the judgment thus criticized, I had pre-announced the number of the final vote (DN 4, p. 60 and DN 5, p. 54; cf 3, 22-23). It was not a prediction but, as always, controlled information. I verified that the numbers published since then by Monsignor Zanic confirmed this expectation—with four exceptions, all the members of this commission were against it.

2. It would be long and tedious to settle here, what the seers could have said, and what one attributes to them. They were very concerned over the sign and they did not stop asking the Virgin when it would come, saying sometimes their suppositions as interpretations, in terms more or less hesitant, and which their interpretors sometimes gave indifferent meanings. To that may be added a well-known factor: the prophetic or eschatological perspective reproaches of the future, through an optical illusion, very well known. Thus Saint Paul thought that the first Christian generation, (and he himself said "us") would see the return of Christ without having gone through death (*1 Thess.* 4:16-17). These illusions, perfectly explainable, do not disqualify them.

AN ARTICLE BY DON AMORTH

In the midst of these uncertainties, information circulated poorly. Father Amorth, Director of "Madre di Dio," which belongs to the same religious family and to the same grand complex of the press as "Famiglia Cristiana" (Msgr. Zanic's tribune), put into circulation this article which he was preparing for "Madre di Dio" in December 1987, (No. 12, p. 15-16). In it, he responded in a clear and strong way to the trouble of many Christians, before the apparent repression or condemnation of the apparitions.

He recalled the considerable evolution of Msgr. Zanic from July 25, 1981, to July 25, 1987, where he guaranteed successively first the sincerity, then the lie of the seers, and the rest.

A qualified canonist, Don Amorth focused on the measures announced by the bishop: "He seems to forbid the celebration of Mass to whomever was favorable to the authenticity of the apparitions, but his statement had not taken the form of a decree; and such a decree would not have been viable nor in conformity with the norms of the Church. The punishment of suspension, through which one forbids a priest to say Mass, would not have been pursued simply on private opinion, nor condemned, or able to be condemned, from the point of view of the faith, morals or freedoms."

Father Amorth underlined certain peculiarities of this venture:

"For six years, I was silent," began Msgr. Zanic, on July 25, 1987. "That is really very much to say," observes Don Amorth. "If there is a man absolutely incapable of remaining silent, a man who has not ceased to speak on Medjugorje, it is Msgr. Zanic: communiques, conferences, interviews to newspapers or to television chains, have been uninterrupted."

"The most resounding case was the dossier of 23 pages which the Bishop of Mostar sent to the press, to all the newspapers, and even to the bookstores on October 30, 1984. The entire text was oriented toward this conclusion: The Bishop of

23

Mostar had seriously considered in a responsible way, the moral certainty that he was dealing with a case of collective hallucinations...The men of science, under the leadership of Professor Servadio, had demonstrated that this conclusion was incoherent:

'One cannot help but be astonished that a bishop has pronounced a diagnosis of a psychiatric kind, in psychiatrically incorrect terms.'

"It was an elegant way of saying that this 'responsible judgment' was incompetent. Further medical exams exclude that it can be considered hallucinations.

"And particularly, these anticipated judgments had a negative repercussion on the Commission of Inquiry, named and presided over by Msgr. Zanic himself. This commission felt itself "scavalcata" (unseated, short-circuited) and dared publish a communique against its president, in which the members ask themselves what meaning their work would have in the future, since the bishop had already pronounced it."

Don Amorth was known as one of the men of the future in the Christian democracy before his religious vocation. He recalled, as an experienced jurist, the dis-credit which the president of a tribunal, who would publish his judgment while preceding the orders in progress, would irrevocably rain upon himself.

He then recalled the last communique that the bishop wanted to publish, in May, 1986, after the commission had been dissolved on orders from Rome, and whose publication Rome impeded. This communique, dated May 19, 1986, transposed the temporary doubt of the majority of the members of the commission, on the supernatural character of Medjugorje, into an apoditic affirmation of the non-supernatural character of these apparitions. He proceeded:

"Since he had repeatedly, short-circuited and up-
rooted the work of his own commission, Msgr. Zanic
tried to short-circuit the competence of the Episcopal Conference (to which one had transferred the
judgment) and that is the reason why the support,
of his colleagues in principal, made him fail to appear at the meeting of September 16. But the greatest
evidence, which this abundance of texts and useless
words (which could have been avoided) imposes,
is the climate of peace, respect and even indestruc-
tible affection for the bishop, which remains the
constant factor in the matter. When I interviewed
the parishoners of Mostar and the seers, I found
echoes of the words of Fr. Tomislav Vlasic, he who
was the most severely and falsely accused by the
bishop:

"He is my bishop, and I must pray for him. I
cannot stand for anyone to speak badly of him."
        (Remarks cited by Don Amorth, ibid, p. 16)

And Father Amorth concludes:
"If you go to Medjugorje, pray with the parishioners and
listen to their testimony; but do not dare say anything evil
of the bishop. They would oppose it, and that, for whoever
knows the character of the Croatians (their sensitivity, their
explosive power of reaction), is a real miracle. . .the real miracle of Medjugorje."

Chapter 3

INQUIRY OF THE EPISCOPAL COMMISSION AND SCIENTIFIC WORKS

The Commission of Inquiry

The Commission founded by the Episcopal Conference under the direction of Msgr. Komarica, Auxilary Bishop of Banja Luka, began its work in March 1987, and held more or less regular meetings every month. Several members of this commission were present on June 25th, the sixth anniversary; very attentive to everything.

A medical inquiry was made in Split on the seers, Maria, Ivan, Vicka and Mirjana, on the 19th and 20th of December 1987, especially by Doctor Korljan (professor of psychiatry in this city). He has the rare characteristic of combining highly technical competence, with an exceptional discernment, including spiritual.

The meetings and works of the Commission were not the object of any communique. Given the tense situation, no longer on the part of the Government, but on the part of the Bishop of Mostar, everything went along in the greatest discretion, which we will respect here (for the same reason). Let us only say that the works of this commission have reached their end. The medical and psychological sub-committee seems to have recognized that the seers were perfectly normal.

What will be the verdict the Episcopal Conference will reach, and from there to the Congregation of the Faith? Let us be on our guard from anticipating it before its publication by Cardinal Kuharic. Custom has it that commissions of inquiry be formed by theologians rather than by spiritual persons experienced in discernment. Now, the predominant perspective among theologians (who are theroticians) has blocked the recognition of apparitions for fifty years. The shedding of tears in Akita (which is basically not an apparition) was recognized by inquiry very much pursued by the bishop, against the warnings of a National Theological Commission.

It then seems difficult, baring a small miracle, for a

commission formed with an overwhelming majority of theologians, to give a positive response to the question: "Has the supernatural been established?"

Initially, the majority would normally answer in a negative or doubtful way (as the first commission), in the absence of geometric or absolute proofs, because that still constitutes our criteria, in use for a half century. An official recognition of the apparitions then, seems relatively improbable, but the value of the scientific arguments (normality of the seers, exceptional miracles) and especially the extent of the spiritual movement of prayer and conversions caused by Medjugorje, would make a negative verdict rather difficult.

The probability then, is that the character of the apparitions and their fruits, as well as the objections, will lead to an endorsement of the pilgrimages without recognition of the authenticity, which could still come at a later time.

The forecast then is much more optimistic than at the time of the first two commissions which Msgr. Zanic headed, beating the drum toward a negative judgment. The new commission has had the merit of rapidly dispatching its work, in a remarkable way for the medical and scientific part. And this commission has had the advantage of working freely, and without confiscation, or blocking of information.

Another progress: Until recently, opposition from the government caused fear on all those who were consulted on the question. How many times, I myself, and all those who wanted to push the investigation, ran into the "language of the forest" which ruled in that country of the east, because religious declarations can cause those, who risk it, to lose their job or their chances for advancement, or their tranquility. On this point, the situation has changed. If it still commands much prudence, one knows that today the economic and tourist authorities of the country would regard the condemnation of Medjugorje as a national catastrophe, and without waiting for an official recognition (unacceptable to the Party) they would wish at least a positive declaration, which is not contrary to continuing this crowd of strangers who come from all parts of the world.

The fact that Monsignor Zanic, the number one opponent,

has been relieved from the case, has also freed the situation; not completely however, since he remains not only a member of the Episcopal Commission, but also the bishop of the place. This gives considerable weight to his judgment, and to his influence, at every stage of this matter. This will also undoubtedly lead one to anticipate a solution of compromise. That solution could be some progress, if it finally permits the parish to work freely and in peace, and not under the threats and perpetual prohibitions, which has been its rule of life until today.

There you have what I think I can say, with respect for all the norms, and the secrets.

PRIVATE MEDICAL STUDIES

I had some regret in seeing published in "Eco" (#49), very well informed, the news that a project of French inquiry, planned at the beginning of January, 1988, had not been able to take place. If it had taken place, it would have also been in the utmost discretion, but it is difficult to "hide a city (such as Medjugorje) located on a mountain," that is to say, a highly spiritual place which causes so much interest, then so much information.

The medical interest in Medjugorje is maintained particularly in Italy. In July, 1985, Professor Cherubino Trabucchi, a member of the International Medical Committee of Lourdes, had proposed to this committee, a study on the events of Medjugorje. Professor T. H. Kammerer, president of the committee, accepted the proposition. In his request, Professor Trabucchi sent him an initial file: reports of Doctors Luigi Frigerio and Giacomo Mattalia, coordinators of the Italian doctors of ARPA. Professor Kammerer worked on a critical report from the Italian work, and those of the French group (recorded in our volume: Henri Joyeux and René Laurentin, "Medical Studies"...), and submitted it for discussion with the International Medical Committee of Lourdes at the time of its session at Lourdes, September 20-21, 1986.

This report was sent to Professor C. Trabucchi, with an invitation to pursue the study. The professor received it with joy.

"On October 20, 1986, at eleven o'clock," his widow wrote to me, "he began reading it. Then, he said to me, 'I will continue this afternoon.' And at 11:50, that same day, a little after the news, he fell asleep in the Lord, without suffering, in his armchair. Our Lady of Medjugorje, in whose apparitions he had believed for a long time, did not want for him to die without this news of his work, which he had prepared with so much love, and the scientific competence which everyone recognized." (Letter of November 11, 1987).

The professor's widow sent me the entire file, of which ARPA had prepared a synthesis. While it deals with a study conducted from a distance, at the request of a foreign colleague, President Kammerer's conclusions are prudent. The philosophical positions of this eminent psychiatrist are situated within the critical current with respect to apparitions and miracles, following that of Professor Lhermite and Father de Tonquedec. He nevertheless concludes in an open manner:

"Nothing is in opposition to the fact that the vision be considered by the Church, as coming from prophetic inspiration (. . .) the last word remains with the Magisterium for the recognition of this supernatural character."

Professor Trabucchi, on his part, envisioned more than one "prophetic inspiration" on the matter; this objective communication with her, who appeared to him.

CURES

With respect to the cures, they continue at Medjugorje. At the end of six and one half years, on March 25, 1988, 339 cures had been spontaneously declared at the parish. And that number is not complete, because the cure of Diana Basile the best study: ("Medical Studies" pages 130-136), and some others did not have the occasion to be declared in the parish. They have been known or studied through other channels, and remain outside this numeration.

Doctor Tonino Antonacci, charged by ARPA (Milan Association for Scientific Research) to set up a permanent operation at Medjugorje as his prospective mission (from January to spring 1987), realized the first sorting out of the most remarkable and best documented cases, some thirty of them.

While waiting for scientific studies, we find at Medjugorje this phenomenon which Doctor de Saint-Maclou, responsible for the verification at Lourdes at the end of the 19th century, called "the miracle of numbers." At Medjugorje, from four to five a month, after more than six years.

It is highly desirable that ARPA continue this scientific enterprise to study them, because the commission, in its legitimate concern to reach some conclusions rapidly, permitting a decision of the Church, is not going to grapple with the entirety of this immense file which would require ten years of studies. Its option would be to confine itself to the study of a conclusive case. Which case will be chosen?

In the current stage of the file, the principal one would seem to be that of Diana Basile: cured instantly of multiple sclerosis, which had existed for twelve years, and which had produced multiple damages, including blindness of the right eye, severe motor problems of four limbs, urinary incontinence. Her complete recovery with no effects, is still more surprising than the instant aspect of her cure. Diana Basile, having been followed closely by the faculty of Milan, benefits from an exemplary file of 150 documents. Professor Spaziante, who pursued the verification for three years, did not find any aftereffects, when the destruction of tissue would have been a normally proper aftereffect. That is one of the extraordinary aspects of this cure.

The difficulty of the diagnosis of multiple sclerosis had not prevented Dr. Thiebaut from recognizing three cures of this illness at Lourdes (Alice Couteault, July 16, 1956), (Leo Schwagerl, December 18, 1960), and (Thea Angel, June 28, 1961). The case of Diana Basile was no less severe, and after a quarter of a century, tests give a superior means of control.

This case seemed then to be the most impressive, with better proofs than those of Lourdes.

In the meantime, the Yugoslavian commission seemed to prefer the case of Damir Coric (#100 in the parish file). Born on July 23, 1960, at Radnik, this young man of 21 years of age, came on January 26, 1982, to declare his cure to Fr. Tomislav Vlasic. Here is the substance of his testimony:

"It is on March 21, 1980, that the long and difficult history of my illness began. For three years previously (thus, at age 16), I felt a weakness in my legs and these symptoms became worse. Examinations begun in Mostar, and completed in Zagreb, led to the diagnosis: 'Internal hydrocephaly with subdural hematoma.' I was operated on five times as the result of repeated complications. When they sent me home on March 6, 1981, I found it absolutely impossible to walk and to eat. I lost the capacity to speak, and my family had to subject me to continuous cleaning in order to relax these sphincters.

"Such was my condition in July 1981. But my family took me by car to Medjugorje, at the foot of the hill of Podbrdo. My mother went up there to pray, and my relatives prayed with perseverance and fasted also. I was able only to do feeble signs with the head, in the absence of words...Meanwhile, I remained conscious. The doctors (who had given up on me) had ceased to help me.

"Approximately three weeks later, they took me again to Medjugorje, as far as the church. There, Vicka prayed over me.

"At that moment, I felt what seemed like a force which was invading me, but in the physical state in which I was, nothing changed. On returning to my home in Buna, I tried to explain with gestures to my mother what I had felt during that prayer. Up to that moment, I could not bend myself sitting down, and at that moment I could. This was the beginning of a gradual improvement, continuous and rapid. Very soon, I took my first step. At Christmas I began to recover my speech. At Easter, the recovery was complete. In October 1983, I went back to work in a factory of compressors in Mostar, and on this occasion, I was declared to be in good health, fit to work at the time of the medical visit."

Doctor Antonacci who visited him at home (in Buna) on May 3, 1987, found him:

"Sane, lucid, in full capacity of intelligence and will, well-balanced, normal in walking and speaking, etc."

The medical commission set up by the Yugoslavian Episcopal Conference has prepared a very remarkable dossier. It is undeniable and verified the poor condition of the sick man, and had justified his return home with a hopeless prognosis.

It is hoped the Commission of Inquiry, concerned about reaching conclusions by taking short cuts, can find in this cure, (or in the two cures recommended) particular evidence in these exceptional files. Also, it is to be wished that the programs started by ARPA continue the study of the phenomena for a long time, as was done at Lourdes, because the miracle of numbers and conversions, sometime bound to these cures, are worthy of pursuit.

For example, let us single out one of the most recent cures: Rita Klaus from Evans City, PA, USA, came in thanks on July 25, 1987, to declare her cure at Medjugorje. The symptoms of multiple sclerosis had begun around 1960, at the moment that she was to make her vows in the religious life. Her condition forced her to leave the convent. She became paralyzed and experienced great pain in her shoulder. She could only move with two crutches or a motorized wheelchair. She practically lived in her wheelchair. But she fought with tremendous energy against her illness. She even married and had children (by cesarian section because of lack of reflexes).

"In February 1986," she testifies, "I read, for the first time, an article on Medjugorje. Immediately, I devoured in one night the book by Laurentin, 'Is the Virgin Mary Appearing in Medjugorje?'

"On June 18, while finishing the Rosary, I heard something like a voice, 'why don't you ask?' Then I began to pray in this manner:

"My dear mother, I believe that you are appearing in Medjugorje. I beg you, ask your Son to cure me and to strengthen my faith.

"I felt like an electrical shock and a great warmth. I fell asleep with a deep sleep. The next morning, I felt this comforting warmth in my legs. I began to move. I put down my crutches, and began to go up and down the stairs rapidly. I ran and cried like a crazy person, crazy with joy. My doctor gave me a lengthy certificate in which he says, among other things, 'The patient has been cured in an extraordinary manner, which I do not know how to explain.'

"My cure has also helped my family. Three brothers and two sisters, who had stayed away from the Church and the Sacraments, have now returned to the practice of their religion."

LUMINOUS PHENOMENA

The luminous phenomena, about which I have gathered a dossier of witnesses, photos and video cassettes, is currently the object of two independent studies.

1. Doctor Fr. Mracek, C.S.C. (Zelena 2, 16000 Prague 6), born on April 12, 1934, is highly specialized in optics and mechanics, and a professor at the Vuzort Institute of Research on the technique of sound and image. He came to Medjugorje for an investigation on the luminous phenomena. He communicated to me his open and judicious conclusions.

They dealt with nine catagories of luminous phenomena, for which he reviews different hypotheses. A natural explanation seems to him, at different degrees, the most probable for half of them; the others remain unexplained and open to an explanation of a supernatural order (see the note at the end of the text, page 37). His conclusion is then, as a last resort, positive.

2. In Italy, a UFO Institute (that is, charged with the study of UFO's: unidentified flying objects) has undertaken a deeper documentary study on the different luminous phenomena of Medjugorje. They asked me for my collaboration which I had envisaged at the beginning. But the UFO name of the group made me fear that this label might assimilate the apparitions of Medjugorje (and related phenomena situated in the orbit of the supernatural) with the discussed, hypothesized and, in every way, natural and cosmic phenomenon of unidentified objects, popularly called "flying saucers." The care to avoid this mistake has kept me, until now, outside of this research in which I recognized and maintained some interest. From the theological and scientific point of view, it is necessary to avoid potential confusion. There is an unassailable barrier between that which comes from supernatural grace (so difficult that there needs to be a study of it) and the natural or semi-natural phenomena which are strictly relevant to the scientific order. The problem is complicated, with classical reservations, with reference to explanations of a parascientific or parapsychological order.

MIRACULOUS WATER AT MEDJUGORJE?

For the same reason, I made every reservation on the very brilliant article of Paola Giovetti, "Dentro l'acqua dei miracoli" (Within the Water of Miracles) based on the studies and declarations of Enza Ciccolo. He was involved in very special research dealing with biology: the water gathered from different holy places would contain remarkable radiations, endowed with therapeutic virtues. Doctor Ciccolo declares particularly:

"I was greatly surprised to establish through the analysis of frequencies, that the water at Lourdes contained seven base vibrations of solar light. The biochemical analysis proved that many pathogenic germs present had lost all their virulence in this environment, just like the water in many other holy places." ("Domenica del Corriere," February 18, 1988, p. 56).

This investigation has led to these conclusions:

"The frequencies which we found in the water at Lourdes invite us to define it as a water of purification, whose action is especially ectodermic, that is to say, it acts in particular on the skin (erythema: irritations, sores, allergies), and on the nervous system...

"The water of Montichiari, just as that of Fatima, is a water of nutrition. Its action is especially endodermal (rather than endothermic, an error of print in the journal, p. 57), that is to say, it acts on the stomach, the intestine, the genitals (menstrual), on the respiratory and cellular nutrition.

"The water of Medjugorje is the water of support and uplifting. Its nature is particularly mesodermic, that is to say, it acts especially on the vertebral column, the muscles, the articulations, the first of innervation on the axial or central parts of man."

All this leads to this final conclusion:

"The fact that in different sacred places there gushes forth waters with diverse therapeutic properties, causes one to envision some intelligent design, a geography which shows a project of grace for man and his environment. Man must only learn to make this project his own, and to utilize these elements of light and harmony to enlighten and balance the earth." (p. 57).

All that leaves me more than dazzled for the following reasons:

1. At Medjugorje, there is no miraculous spring, and no water is utilized in the pilgrimage nor recommended by the Blessed Virgin as presenting particular characteristics.

2. Examinations carried on at a very advanced level, which have been made on all the possible radiations at Medjugorje, did not manifest any remarkable peculiarity. Professor Lipinski (*Medical Studies*, p. 126), who had documented astonishing numbers, was not able to personally verify these first measures which were improvised (since his equipment was seized by the Yugoslav police who forbade him to stay), and these numbers were invalidated by later research.

3. It seems unfortunate to us, methodologically as well as theologically, to reduce the miracles, free acts of God, to some physical properties (unknown and assumed) of earthly elements. This presupposition also seems to be of little benefit for scientific research as well as theological discernment, because it counts on hypotheses which are favorable to language, but which escape verification. One still lacks the adequate criteria to state precisely to what extent the natural and the supernatural are identified, are different, and are clearly stated.

Mankind is always too inclined to reduce the latter to the former.

THE STUDY OF DOCTOR-FR. MRACEK

Here, in brief, is the state of the conclusions of Dr. Mracek, dated in 1987, though it is understood that his study is ongoing.

CROSS AT KRIZEVAC

The first three categories of facts, concern the cross of Krizevac, situated on the hill which overlooks Medjugorje:

1. Certain persons have perceived the unexplained "rotation" which has been recorded on film. Mracek refers here to our volume "Medical Studies." He envisages some natural explanations (geometric aberration, play of solar rays), without concluding precisely on this point.
2. Obliteration of the cross at Krizevac, in which observers were astonished to see it disappear. He envisions a similar hypothesis on this matter, without any conclusions.
3. The image of Our Lady, which appeared on photographs, near the cross at Krizevac. Here, he does not envisage the possibility of special effects (which may merit consideration for certain comparisons) and considers unlikely, an explanation influenced by psycho-physical fields, studied by the American Ted Serias.

OPTIC PHENOMENA

4. Luminous phenomena around the church of Medjugorje. He refers (as we did ourselves), the photos which we had published in "Medical Studies," to the diffraction of light. The largest opening of the diaphragm favors the phenomena of diffraction.
5. The image of the crucified Christ on the bosom of the statue of the apparitions ("Medical Studies"). He thinks that this cross is explained through the play of reflected lights. Dr. Mracek does not seem to have examined the problem raised by our book. One is astonished at seeing the image of the cross formed in very different conditions of lighting; i.e., picture taken from the front, in flash, where the image is sharper, and a picture taken under a diffused natural light.

SIGNS IN THE HEAVEN

6. Solar rotation a little before sunset. He explains this phenomenon (as we did ourselves) as a common illusion of an optic nature due to the overradiation and the fatigue of the retina. A phenomena which can be explained, although it is not the object of a specific text. But other phenomenon, not reducible to this explanation, continued to be a problem. (R. Laurentin and R. Lejeune, "Message and Teachings of Mary at Medjugorje, Chronological Corpus of the Messages.")

7. The appearance of the word MIR (peace) in the sky in 1981. One knows that a picture had been taken of this phenomenon, but it was confiscated. (ibid, p. 71). Dr. Mracek, who does not know these precise details, as well as the dates, eliminates the explanation through the laser; that would demand a "gigantic" source which does not appear either likely or verified.

8. The apparition of the figure of a woman on the hill of the apparitions. (Mentioned by L. Rupic, "Gospina Samobor," 1983) according to the testimony of d'Umberto Loncar (S. Kraljevic: "Les Apparitions de Medjugorje," 1984). Doctor Mracek does not see in it, in principal, any explanation of a natural order.

9. The figure of a woman seen by sixty witnesses on Krizevac, according to the testimonies cited in R. Laurentin, "Is The Blessed Virgin Appearing in Medjugorje?" Having taken into account the state of good health of the witnesses (approximately sixty), Doctor Mracek does not have, in principal, any satisfactory natural explanation.

His study, which would be called "continuation and complementary," recognized the natural explanation which is imposed for a part of nine cases which had been documented. It does not see any explanation for the others, which he considers as open to the explanation of a supernatural order.

Chapter 4

CONTROVERSIES

One must speak of the psycho-medical critique of Medjugorje by Pier Angelo Gramaglia, object of two books:

"Towards a Marian Revival?" (Verso un Rilancio Mariano?—Torino, ed. Claudiana, 1985.)
"The Ambiguity of Medjugorje: Marian Apparitions or Mediumistic Phenomenon?" (L'equivoco di Medjugorje: Apparizioni Mariane O Fenomeni di Medianita?—Torino, ed. Claudiana, 180 pg. 1987).

The author tries to explain Medjugorje as a "mediumistic phenomenon." That means a case of "altered conscience," evolving into "auto or self-hypnosis" (the ambiguity, p. 27-28), with "the externalization of paranormal facilities" (p. 62), induced by "the great manipulator, Tomislav Vlasic," (Gramaglia uses here the terms of Monsignor Zanic). Briefly, it would deal "with a disconcerting fare of hallucinations integrated into the faith."

The author is neither a doctor nor a psychiatrist. He is a theologian, Professor of Patristic Theology at Turin, but he has some very well-refined medical and psychological acquaintances from whom he undoubtedly benefited. And he expounds them with skill and clarity. We will keep his objections and present hypotheses because every objection invites further interest in the medical/psychological studies. More new tests would be useful to better exclude these unfounded hypotheses.

If every intelligent objection stimulates research, these two books do not disturb what we have already established. The reader deserves to know:

1. Gramaglia did not meet the seers nor examine the ecstasies. Now, in this matter, the clinical observation and the profound knowledge of the persons and of the environment are critical. One cannot judge by the exterior alone.

Gramaglia, with no personal observation, builds on what
he has not seen.
2. His method, though brilliant, is essentially controversial.
3. As with every controversy, it is inspired by an ideology.
This ideology is dependent on the idealistic philosophy
still prevalent, even in Catholic universities and seminaries. It tends to systematically explain facts through subjectivity rather than objectivity, and to regard as a hoax,
or pathology, everything which seems an encounter in tan-
gible reality in the Christian faith, such as the Resurrection of Christ. In the idealistic perspective, this Resurrection
would be a matter of faith alone, and would not have
been able to leave any impressions. That is why one of
Gramaglia's first targets has been the Shroud of Turin (1978
and 1981).

His other controversies were aimed at the Charismatic
Renewal and the mystics such as Maria Valtorta or Fr. Gobbi,
founder of the Marian Movement of Priests. Other targets included the Genoese journalist Gianni Baget Bozzo (in one
of the chapters in "Toward a Renewal"), the Jehovah Witnesses (1984), and the Mormons (1985).

In "The Ambiguity of Medjugorje," he clearly expresses
the ideology which guides his polemics. He excludes, as a
myth, (p. 165) the possibility of having some "sensorial experiences of the Divine world," as expounded, he says, "in
the Charismatic Movement," and "the demagogy of the media
managed and controlled by Communione Liberazione." Those
things, he claims, would be only artificial and dangerous means
in order to promote:

> "A Catholic identity of the masses, an anti-
> conciliar clerical revenge, nostalgic of devotional-
> ism (. . .) which the Catholic Bourgeoisie, willing
> to abundantly finance this propaganda, crowned by
> the Wojtilien support, produces ecclesiastic mani-
> festations capable of providing a spectacle, and
> especially of being filmed by television." (P. 165).

One of the weaknesses of this militant enterprise, so sure of itself, is to be selective and to caricature the authors who are implicated, (in my own case, the manner in which I am cited). Gramaglia skillfully gathered some isolated details, in order to construct a systematic program.

A strange and fascinating established fact: Gramaglia's polemic of the left has striking resemblances and similarities with the polemic of the right—of the Catholic counter-reformation. These two polemics, diametrically opposed in their fundamental goals, have the same merits: intelligence, brilliance, erudition, confidence in their hypotheses, selectivity in documentation. They likewise feel as useless, the need to go to see that which they are talking about. Their ideology and the citations which they have acquired from books, furnish material more favorable for their comeback. The strangest thing is that these polemics attack the same targets—the apparitions at Medjugorje, Charismatic Renewal, and Pope John Paul II, for reasons paradoxically opposed. The counter-reformation excommunicates him as a heretic, a grave digger of Catholic dogma; and Gramaglia censors him for strengthening this dogma and the fruitful convictions which result from it.

The main faults with the polemics is their simplification, their selectivity, and especially the unproductiveness that results from it. That is why it is no place on which to waste one's time. Life is short, and the study of great questions (including Medjugorje) progresses by experimental, modest, progressive approaches concerned with the complete understanding of reality, in opposition to clever polemics, and just draining substance from the object. All those who have seriously studied the facts of Medjugorje, medical or spiritual, have felt to have surpassed beyond all basic areas, a little like the physicists studying the inexhaustible riches and resources of the atom.

It is beautiful what one feels for the experience of the seers, its coherence, holiness, the impressive number of conversions, and spiritual, psychic and physical cures. Those factors forbid simple reductions, and requires the respectful approach of every authentically scientific study. It is at this level that we shall continue to place the balance sheets, beyond polemics.

This scientific concern for honesty, which goes from hypotheses to verification, not without refinements and corrections, seems to recall focusing in on an ambiguous phrase from our medical studies, (pg. 97) which tends to lend itself to an objection for overestimation. This phrase seems to say that the electro-encephalograms of the seers in ecstasy excluded hallucination.

If such was our conclusion, it would be incorrect. Let us stress then what has been inadequately expressed.

1. The ambiguous phrase stated clearly that the electro-encephalogram excludes "paroxysistic hallucination." This (imprecise) expression is aimed only at extreme cases, the type of hallucination which one finds in acute stages of epilepsy (effectively excluded by the electro-encephalogram).
2. The ambiguous phrase on page 97 had been left in its imprecision with reference to what had previously been said in our same work (p. 65): that what the electro-encephalogram formerly excluded were sleep, dreams, and epilepsy. One can only exclude hallucination on the cross-checking of those which have been given with "clinical observation." And it is this point that we would like to clarify if the seers, tired of so many exams, were to again agree to allow themselves to be subjected to more advanced tests in the laboratory.

It also seems to us that Professor Servadio (Italian) has rightly excluded "collective hallucinations," and that hallucinations, prolonged for a period of seven years, would in some way, have destroyed the equilibrium of the seers. He continued on this thesis. In an impressive way, he has shown the difficult, and even impossible conditions of life, which would have resulted after seven years—their communications, their social relations, etc.

And yet, it is the opposite which has been verified year after year. It suffices that the medical commission of Medjugorje, for a long time prejudiced against the claimed psychic equilibrium problem of Vicka, through certain studies in meeting her during two hours on February 26, 1988, verified her equilibrium and the futility of the suspicions which had been hastily concluded.

CANADA: BELANGER-SIVRIC

Another attack against Medjugorje comes to us from Canada; an attack of some weight, since it begins with a book of 400 pages, which will be followed by a second one. Responsible for the work is Louis Belanger. He will be the author of the second volume, and he is the French translator and the editor of the first volume written by Father Ivo Sivric ("The Hidden Face of Medjugorje #1," Ed. Psilog, Saint Francois du Lac).

Louis Belanger, born in Quebec in 1921, a student of political sciences, who later studied in Germany (Fribourg) what one calls parapsychology, which no university official recognized and integrated among its official disciplines. That is why Belanger prefers to title this work, a study of "paranormal phenomena."

Louis Belanger is a vigorous and capable man. Each time that I have had to deal with him, he is preceded by friends or emissaries who made impressive eulogies about him. Without having a university doctorate and without apparently being either practicing or relieving, he is in charge of the course and the faculty of Theology at Montreal. He is excellent in publicity. He knows how to pass along on American and European radios his meager research on haunted houses or identification of unknown causes, and he has already made known his attacks against Medjugorje in an aerial broadcasting of Antenna 2, beginning 1988.

Louis Belanger made a unique and short trip to Medjugorje in January 1985 during the severe winter which interrupted every pilgrimage. He retained a recollection of it as "a frozen desert." Monsignor Zanic, who helps and stimulates the opponents, generally opened his archives to him. Since June 1985, Belanger has been publishing in *Chatelaine* (monthly magazine from Montreal) his hasty conclusions, the "tectonic movements" of the:

"mountains and rocks which move by cycle, and
relieves the pieso-electrical or geomatic effects which
manifest themselves under the form of columns of
light and [. . .] can influence the behavior of the
living organism. This electromagnetic light, while
passing through the temporal lobe [. . .] releases
visions which they have interpreted according to their
culture [. . .]. The children of Medjugorje have really
seen a luminous phenomenon which they have interpreted, according to their culture, as being the
Gospa. What else could they see, these young people, raised in the faith and the culture of Mary whose
month had just ended?" (p. 62)

Belanger disqualifies Fr. Slavko Barbaric, Doctor in Psy-
chology and author of a memoir on the seers, because "he
believed." His study is then unfortunately "subjective" (p. 48).
Let us take note of this presupposition which Belanger confided during an interview: "Faith would be incompatible with
the objectivity of science. Only a study which gave a natural
explanation, foreign to faith, would be objective. Scientific
thesis forbids God to make miracles in this place; it forbids
Christ and the Blessed Virgin from manifesting themselves,
since they are only myths."

The interview of *Chatelaine* slandered me. Belanger had
made it impossible for me to meet him before going to Medjugorje, in spite of my offer of "an introduction" which I
gave him on the assurance that he was working in open objectivity, as a "professor of a faculty of theology." The calumnies
are numerous in the interview. Among others, I think "the
judgment of Doctor Mangiapan" should have been omitted.
I also had consulted Dr. Mangiapan on the cures in Medjugorje. It should have been omitted because it presented only
the negative aspect. I had previously published it in its entirety, according to both aspects, positive and negative conclusions, and it is my adversaries who cheat in publishing only
the negative part. I wrote to Belanger, and also to "Chatelaine:"
"If you are honest, correct these errors." I received no response.

In the course of several trips to Canada, I asked Belanger to receive me as I had received him (in inviting him to breakfast). I was unsuccessful. Some Canadian friends advised me against insisting. They said, "you will not get anywhere with those people who do not have a good reputation among us. Legal proceedings would only demean you."

Belanger had the opportunity to meet a Croatian Franciscan, born at Medjugorje: Ivo Sivric, born in 1917. I had also contacted this Franciscan, (due to the fact that he was born in Medjugorje, not because he was supposedly a "theologian" as the propaganda said. He simply had studied to become a priest in the seminary at Mostar.) I had sought to gather his points of view. But he kindly avoided my repeated letters. In fact, he was already allied to Belanger and wanted to disseminate information only under this negative aspect and did not wish to reveal his intentions.

Father Sivric, unlike Belanger, had the credit of taking three trips to Medjugorje. As an opponent, he was received with open arms by Monsignor Zanic, who opened his archives to him and communicated his point of view to the priest. One finds then, in his book, the majority of discrepancies which Monsignor Zanic had disseminated about persons favorable to Medjugorje, myself included. I will not return to that because I have contradicted these in my previous book ("Latest News #2"), but Father Sivric ignored this work, which no one has ever contested. Let us leave there the debacle which raged in the Balkan quarrels of Mostar.

Father Sivric had the talent to sort the errors and falsehoods spread by the bishop, especially when they concerned his colleagues, whom he had fraternally cared for. He who accuses me of omissions, also omitted reporting the (false) accusations of the bishop, against a Franciscan. He said almost nothing of the difficult situation there, contrary to the usage and constitution of this Franciscan order. There, the Franciscan province of Mostar was maintained, and whose former Provincial, who had been deposed, died in exile. Also not explained was the legal proceedings of the two Franciscans, whom he incriminates, and of the bishop's revision of the "Tribunal of

the Apostolic Signature," (which in the Church is the same
as a Supreme Court of Appeal).[1]

Let us speak instead, about the merits of Father Sivric. He
published and translated numerous interviews of the seers
recorded from the first days, and gathered on tape by Monsignor Zanic and his commission. I do not ignore these cassettes, I use them step-by-step in my book "Account of the
Apparitions" and, moreover, having had them translated by
some Croatian friends, have proof that these interviews were
carried out in dramatic and distressing conditions. Things were
getting too much for seers and priests, the crowd, the work-
load, the fatigue, fear of the police. The seers defended themselves as best they could, facing the skepticism of priests who
were right in being critics. From it, came interrupted dialogue, many questions without answer or with answers without significance. Indeed there were minor contradictions, as
there always are in similar cases. I was reassured that Father
Sivric himself often interrupted this transcribing by noting
"incomprehensible" (99 times for the interview of June 20th).
One can only congratulate him then for having deciphered
and edited conscientiously these trying interviews. Such is
the first page of Vicka's diary edited by her sister Anna (p.
237-246). Whoever has a critical sense can pry from these
spontaneous interviews some useful elements, as I have tried
to do in "Account." Fr. Sivric apparently sorted out especially what he found negative against the authenticity of the
apparitions.

The author had the courage to prepare a bibliography of
200 titles of printed books, manuscripts, etc., which he com-
piled in an alphabetical order of authors. This establishes the
basis of his sources, but also its limits. He did not know,
for example, of half of my works. So I wondered why he
accused me of "flagrant omissions" which he attributes to
hidden intentions. It is simply because I say elsewhere what
he did not manage to find at random.

The numerous Croatian documents which he translated in
the course of his work, will provide a service to all specialists,
even if the worth is characterized by a double translation,

from Croatian to English by Father Sivric, and from English
to French by L. Belanger. Included, among other things, is
Monsignor Zanic's sermon dated July 25th, 1987, reproduced
in that volume, but evidently not the answer by Fr. Ivan
Dugandzic. (See appendix page 100).

Briefly, the author is sincere and conscientious, but he uses
his tremendous documentation toward one end only, the negative. Others, hopefully myself included, have covered these
points but without becoming buried in insignificant details.
Seeing this polarization of the signs, or negative hypothesis,
one is astonished that the balance sheet is so light.

What is sad in this book is that everything is exaggerated.
Some small details become enormous and are repeated, turned
over in one's mind, indefinitely, to produce a negative impact
on the reader. The negative testimony or overwhelming mis-
fortune, which the author gathered at Medjugorje, is sometimes
conditional, and is a form of insinuation, sometimes without
a place or date, or anything which permits its verification.

The reputation of the people cited is either clear or obscur,
according to whether they took up the negative point of view
of Bishop Zanic, or they dared to maintain a different point
of view, open to criticism. Bishop F. Franic, Archbishop of
Split: (he who had Zanic promoted to the episcopacy and who
is president of the Doctrinal Commission of the Yugoslav Episcopacy, after having been a member of the Doctrinal Commission of the Council) was treated as "a dissenter." Here,
an error of translation undoubtedly took place. With my experience of the critique of the text, I have the feeling that
Belanger's translation hardened and polemicized Father Sivric's
words, whose intentions were peaceful. I would not be surprised if the extremist terms used in opposition to me, are
also the act of the translator, rather than that of Father Sivric.

Especially painful, in this regard, is the chapter on the credibility and the moral value of the "seers," whom the translator
calls the "visionaries" (in French this word means "false seers,"
in English it is neutral in its meaning.) What Father Sivric
claims against them is really insignificant. Some anonymous
witnesses found fault with the fact that the seers did not respond

to their greetings. But thousands of people greet them at one and the same time in the course of days. How could they answer to all and to each one individually? Their difficulties or their silence before a barrage of diverse and fallacious questions are interpreted as calculating, by some interviewers. While answering a thousand questions, they have to keep their secrets, discretion and respect for people. For that, Father Sivric does not find anything to accuse them of, but because of their escape from so many traps and indiscretions, he found them evasive and liars. They are no more liars than any other person from the Mediterranean, including Father Sivric himself, in his own one-sided way of presenting the event. Fr. Sivric's presentation is systematic and passionate, even if one sided, but it would be rude, false, and insulting to call it deceitful.

If Fr. Sivric does not take up in detail the most vile accusation hurled against Father Tomislav Vlasic (and I will admire him for this discretion, rather than call it "a flagrant omission"), he assumes an accusation of "perjury" by the Bishop of Mostar against Tomislav Vlasic, as akin to damnation. This word "PERJURY" appears in capital letters in the title of the chapter, and returns to it in every page, at least in the running heading without the accusation finding any basis. On the other hand, the author does not say anything of the many contradictions by Father Radogost Grafenauer, S.M., one of the first advisors of the bishop. Monsignor Zanic depends essentially on his testimony to affirm, in his name, that Vicka keeps a hidden diary, that she had lied on this point, and that Tomislav Vlasic had been perjurer on this point. But Father Grafenauer did not cease contradicting this interpretation, contrary to his original intentions and to the truth. ("Dernieres Nouvelles" #4 pg. 83, #5 pgs. 50-54).

The following chapters (8 to 10, pgs. 115-166) defend the negative point of view of Monsignor Zanic, and one cannot be surprised. And, one is always right in taking up in defense of a bishop, but the author would have done better to more curtail, than increase, the abusive accusations and calumnies against his adversaries.

The book emerges as a very disarming attempt to explain how it all happened. (Chapter 11, p. 167). It says that Mirjana read a book on Lourdes in 1981, and from there, she would have done an imitation of Lourdes and the stage would then be set. Father Sivric establishes that point on two or three mentions of Lourdes during more than 150 pages of interrogatory. I have taken that into account in my book "Accounts" (p. 51). This suggestion is totally insignificant. Medjugorje is not a copy of Lourdes in any way. These young people did not look for a grotto, or for water (though there was some). The message is not an imitation of the message of Lourdes. The author, who has little experience in scientific hypotheses, allowed himself to be led to crystallize everything around a single detail.

The most disarming thing of the role of a theologian is that he honestly recognize (like everyone, including Monsignor Zanic), the marvelous fruits of this event at Medjugorje and more broadly in the world: "The faithful of Medjugorje are authentically very religious and very spontaneous in their faith," says the author, Fr. Sivric (p. 176). But he adds:

> "We can then imagine what effect this [fervent] environment can produce on the pilgrims which come from all corners of the world where the faith has lost its attraction and its force [. . .]. It is easy to understand that other people are involved in every movement which begins to live intensely from this fervor. Belief then feeds on belief. Like a fire it spreads from itself, but who will believe that it is the Blessed Virgin who is lighting it?"

The author has the good sense to recognize that everything is not able to be the work of the devil. But his explanation for "the fire" makes one think of that of the doctor in Moliere: "That is why your daughter is mute."

What is rather sad is that he forgets to state precisely what he recognizes as globally admirable, and to utilize the criterion of Christ himself in the Gospel: *You will know the tree by its fruits.* He recognizes that the fruits are good, but adds immediately that the fact of the apparition "is false, of course."

If the faith of his native village has suddenly become capable of mobilizing up to 150 confessors a day, amazed to find more conversions in one afternoon than they have found during their entire life; if there are so many healings which the author eliminates with the stroke of the pen; if prayer and fasting have taken such strides because of Medjugorje on an international level, is it really necessary to work desperately hard to put out this fire? Father Sivric's zeal is sincere, thus laudable in intention. We find in it this same passionate ardor which apparitions inspire in ideologies both of the right and of the left, as mentioned above.

When the Blessed Virgin appears, not all of the family circle applauds loudly. In his arsenal, he looks for all the means necessary to reduce this Lady to mythology and to subjectivity. In spite of my scientific background, I prefer to this "phenomena of rejection," the naivete (the clarity) of Catherine Laboure saying, when she learned of the apparitions of Lourdes: "It is the same one." And I think that I have good reason to say the same thing in seeing the fruits of Medjugorje, and the seers themselves so sadly criticized in that book. It suffices to open one's eyes and heart in order to admire the marvelous teaching of Our Lady, and to catch a glimpse of her, transparently, as I see her through Bernadette, and through the seers at Medjugorje.

In recent months the controversy has been unleashed in the United States, spurred by the mobilizing action of Belanger/Sivric. There seems to be a convergence to destroy Medjugorje and its supporters. More often than not, it is with arguments from the right, in some respects opposed to those from the left, as from Belanger/Sivric. One can now place a bibliography:

"Critiques of Medjugorje"—Br. James, S.D.B., 650 Filbert St., San Francisco, CA 94133. (A 47 page memoir which has been widely disseminated.)

"Medjugorje A Warning"—Michael Davies, in "The Remnant," May 31, 1988. (Which reproduces the sermon of Msgr.

Zanic of July 1987, along with a letter of support by Msgr. Zanic.)

"Medjugorje—The Untold Story"—Michael Jones, Fidelity Magazine, September 1988, pgs. 18-44 and October 1988, pgs. 20-36.

PUBLISHERS FOOTNOTE

1. A published response to "The Hidden Face of Medjugorje" has also been written by a Yugoslavian priest, Fr. Ljudevit Rupcic. A copy can be obtained on request from The Riehle Foundation.

The author, Fr. Laurentin, with Vicka

Chapter 5

THE FRUITS

The fruits of Medjugorje are the best proof of the authenticity of the apparitions, which continue. They are developing, and they are deepening.

It would be tedious to take up again the enumeration of the different lines of the fruits pointed out in *"Latest News, No. 6"* and in *"Messages and Teachings of Mary at Medjugorje."* One of the most striking facts is the continued growth of pilgrimages, in spite of the worldwide warning, through the indictment by Monsignor Zanic. The pilgrimages from Italy, where the shock was the greatest, have suffered a decrease.

The situation is comparable in France where the influence of the press, including the Catholic press, is silent or negative with respect to Medjugorje.

But the increase in pilgrimages is very strong in a number of countries: Primarily the United States, Austria and Germany, which have greatly surpassed France in spite of the distance. The same with Canada.

It is no longer a question of curiosity, because everything has been done to separate it. The pilgrims who come no longer hope to attend the ecstasies, although they are more and more discreet and often without witnesses. The great daily liturgy is in the Croatian language and of an extreme length, approximately three hours. In discomfort, the great majority remain standing and crowded. It is astonishing that people, without special training in prayer, support these marathons without impatience, and without an identifiable incentive. An unexplainable grace maintains them inwardly.

CONVERSIONS

For a long time, I have regretted that the effort made to gather information on the cures has not been applied to conversions, a record of a still more significant religious interest. The accounts are legendary and often anonymous, as a matter of discretion. We shall give sporadic samples of them in the following chapter: Testimony.

THE SEERS

The fruits of the apparitions continue to be remarkable among the seers themselves. Nothing had commanded their attention up to that first moment. They had their qualities and their faults, as they themselves recognize. They were ingenuous, but impressionable and fragile. Today, they display a great personal and spiritual quality. Some of them have reached unbelievable heights, such is evident in the case of Maria.

At the time of my trip, at the end of March 1988, I was caught up by the deep spirituality of Vicka. No more impatience but an untiring serenity, a willingness to accept anything that befell her, giving of herself completely at each moment. Her capacity to listen increased her facing the uninterrupted stream of hundreds of pilgrims who visit her every day. She is placid listening to the Italians, from whom she learns the language intuitively. She tirelessly signs autographs without shortening her name to initials, as I suggested it to her. Her personal warmth and smile become more and more transparent. She has received every visitor as a privileged friend. The visitor keeps this impression. All this comes from a total forgetfulness of herself, and a complete abandonment to Our Lady, her guide.

Without ever deviating from perfect tact and correctness, Vicka receives without reservation, beyond her human strength. Let us cite some testimony, among others:

> "She is everything to the pilgrims. She forgets to eat, and to rest.
> —'Narod caka' (the people are waiting) she says. And she leaves the dining table to receive those who in successive waves invade the little courtyard of her home. She communicates to them the messages of the Gospa, answers their questions, agrees to autographs, allows herself to be photographed and to be embraced. She shakes hands, smiles at everyone,

and is happy to make others happy." (Public testimony in "Eco," No. 45, p. 11).

She has the same simple, direct, unceremonious contact with
the Ambassador from the United States, Alfred H. Kingon
(who came to Medjugorje for two weeks to pray for the healing of his son), or with a young American, sick with AIDS,
who asked her to embrace him, which she did while saying:

> "God will not give me the sickness of another
> person, since I only want what is good for him.
> After six years with so many embraces, how many
> illnesses would I have caught!"

She stops everything for the sick, the handicapped. For
several years, young drug addicts, undergoing treatment for
their dependency, were led to Medjugorje by Sr. Elvira (Italian). For Vicka, they are an object of her predilection. She
had gone to visit them in Italy. On September 3, 1987, for
her 23rd birthday, she made herself beautiful and spent the
evening with them, from nine o'clock until midnight, with
songs, games, and pictures. She is loved by these young people, as a sister and an angel. Her freedom, spontaneity, her
ability to welcome people, are extraordinary.

She has suffered the aftereffects of this devouring life, but
they are part of her vocation, the heavy part of the Cross of
Christ, which is hers. It is the hidden face of Vicka. The Lord
asked her for that, as a price for all the good that she does.
Maria, who had found her to be imprudent, and sympathized
with this annoying test to her health, admired the results:

"Vicka has surprised me very much," she recently stated.

With her wisdom, fragility and prudence, Maria would hardly
state less. But she would agree in a more limited, more reflec-
tive way. Her radiance is also great. Her deep spirituality,
her simplicity, her transparency exceed every expression. One
could guess at what price she endures (with a smile) this su-
perhuman tension. But she was very happy that Tomislav invited her to this "desert" of privacy and prayer in Italy, for

which she left on February 28th, until the beginning of August 1988. (See the Chronology).

With Ivan, one perceives an analogous growth, deep and discreet. He continues to greatly influence his prayer group and each Monday this group climbs one of the two hills, Podbrdo or Krizevac, for a long vigil, usually with an apparition at the end. Ivan's personality is not suited to the constant badgering of those who come, and this is sometimes mistaken as a lack of interest on his part. He is a young man of deep, private spirituality.

The three other seers are more discreet than secret.

Mirjana continues her studies at Sarajevo. Her friend, who seems to be her fiance for two years, has, like she, abandoned his former studies, and both are doing studies in economics. Like Ivanka, she seems to be oriented towards marriage, but in a different social environment. She and Marc, like the rest of her family, fast on bread and water once a week. This is not so easy in the hectic life of a large city. Her prayer, her reflection and mission, are a contrast to the atheists of the environment in which she lives, and where she has valiantly undergone the test. Her messages are often characterized by apocalyptic perspectives which, in many respects, are appropriate to her. She did not have any new apparitions after the one on her birthday, March 18, 1987, but only locutions. After August 1987, she received two locutions each month. On March 18, 1988, the annual apparition on her birthday, promised by Our Lady, was fulfilled and lasted approximately 12 minutes. It was in Sarajevo, in the presence of her family and numerous friends. The revelation of the secrets which had been promised, and of which she will confide the disclosure to Father Pero, has not progressed.

Ivanka is blossoming in her vocation as a wife and mother. Her desire for a family was delayed and tried for a long time, but along with much joy and tenderness, seriousness and discernment, in her prayers. Now, the Mass, Rosary, morning and evening prayers, suffice for her Christian life, where neither meditation nor special devotions are added. But prayer penetrates her life. During Lent, 1988, she fasted entirely on bread and water according to a local tradition, except on Sunday (because Sunday is not Lent). With her husband, she goes for a long period of prayer, each week on the hill.

"Little Jakov," who is now big, vigorous and more and more enthralled with football, has acquired depth in personal prayer, without considering himself responsible for the mission of welcoming pilgrims as Maria and Vicka.

PRAYER GROUPS

The prayer groups, which have multiplied in the parish of Medjugorje, are the most significant points of growth in the parish, the apex of its life. They have been imitated and have spread around the world. In Medjugorje, it enables dozens of persons to be entirely abandoned to, and willingly consecrated to God without reserve.

THE RISE OF NEW RELIGIOUS FAMILIES

Around Tomislav Vlasic (In the Appennines)

The members of one of these prayer groups (the one which used to meet in the basement of the presbytery) had promised, on the request of the Blessed Virgin, not to make any commitment or decision involving their future for four years.

Tomislav Vlasic came unexpectedly and discreetly to Medjugorje a little after the end of these four years, on November 15 to 22, 1987, and according to the program then established, he led, on February 26th, 1988, a group of 15 to northern Italy for a long spiritual retreat of five months (March to July), completely devoted to prayer. This hermitage, which included notably the seer Maria, her American friend Kathleen, Maria Dugandzic, etc., will probably result in a decision for the establishment of a Croatian community, possibly in Medjugorje. The place of this retreat remains confidential in order to protect the privacy: "In Italy, in the Appennines," is all that is stated. But the vacuum created in Medjugorje by the absence of Maria arouses the ingenuity of so many Italians, that the secret progressively transforms itself into a discretion which is very difficult to maintain. The community will undoubtedly be required to leave.

The composition of this community of prayer will permit one to predict the characteristics of the new religious family, which will undoubtedly be born: a mixed group, (boys and girls) with a new style, founded on prayer, in sustained dialogue with God in all profoundness and creativity. That can have great consequences for the future of the Church, as did the rise of the Franciscans at the turning point of the 12th and 13th Centuries.

Around Gianni Sgreva, at Priabona

What is the relationship between this group, directed by Tomislav Vlasic, and a new religious community which begins in a like manner, also in Italy in Vicenza, and similarly to live the message of Medjugorje as a total consecration founded on prayer?

It would be premature to state precisely. But one has the feeling that in spite of the identity of inspiration, of plan, of goal, of community structures, founded on Medjugorje, the two foundations, which could unite, will maintain their independence. Vocations will not be lacking to neither the one nor the other. The problem, on the contrary, is the excessive number of people wanting to join.

Gianni Sgreva, a young Italian priest, a Passionist Religious, a theologian and a qualified Biblical scholar (he taught at the major seminary of Verone), first began his foundation at Priabona, in the Diocese of Vicenza (in Northern Italy) in May 1987.

The increase is such that he envisioned transferring his community for lack of space to receive the vocations which were joining. I was there in November 1987, at the time of the first telephone call on this matter. The religious from Saint-Gaetan (not far from Priabona), where the monastery had become too large for lack of vocations, proposed to him a more suitable place. It may happen, new space has become necessary.

I have transcribed below what Gianni Sgreva told me of the project; which he wrote to me in a memo and by his statements to the editor of the journal *"Eco,"* which has followed this matter extremely well.

"How was this idea of a community of devoted people born?" I had asked Gianni Sgreva.

"The plan dates back to the second half of July 1985. I was staying at the home of Maria Pavlovic. We spoke of the consecration which the Gospa asked of her. And the desire took hold of me to give substance to this new spiritual life in a permanent way, a group which would live this adherence to God through Mary. One day, when I was working in the tobacco fields with Maria, she said to me:

'Where will I go after the apparitions? Which congregation or institute will be able to follow the education which the Gospa has given for four years (since the beginning of the apparitions)?'

"The plan rooted itself in the concern of finding again the inspiration of the apostolic age, according to the Acts of the Apostles. The eleven: *devoted themselves to constant prayer, together with some women, and Mary, the Mother of Jesus, and his brothers. (Acts: 1,14).* It is in the high chamber, this cenacle, that the Church was born in the waiting for the Holy Spirit. Mary guided this waiting. There were there, not only the Apostles (the origin of the bishops and the priests), but also some lay people, men and women: the whole Church in its infancy. Medjugorje, the world movement, which interests the whole Church, invites one to find a form of consecration where all the original components of the Church are found again, in sharing the experience of the cenacle, guided by Mary, as she is at Medjugorje. Such was the first and embryonic line which was taking shape.

"That same day we visited an Orthodox monastery in Mostar. It clarified our reflection. The structure of this place embodied what we were looking for: at the center was a church dedicated to Mary, with two main parts of the building, on each side; the one was occupied by monks, the other (on the left) by nuns. Life was centered on the little church of the Madonna. Then why couldn't others live together, men and women, celibate and married, desiring to reconstruct the primitive cenacle guided by Mary toward a new Pentecost?"

The project seemed utopian, but the signs came at the meeting.

"In December 1985," continued Gianni Sgreva, "I was in Medjugorje and that evening I had given up going to the apparition in order to hear confessions. And thus, after Mass, Maria approached me and said:
    —'Do you know that the Madonna talked to me about you?'
    —'What,' I asked, astonished, 'What did she tell you?'
    —'I cannot tell you yet, but only when you are in an environment of meditation.'
"The following day, December 5th, at her house, after a long time of prayer, she confided to me this message. I had trouble believing it and for that reason I asked her to write the statements from the Madonna, in Croatian language, so that I could have it translated by Slavko in order to avoid the risks of subjectivism. Father Slavko confirmed the meaning of the message which said this: 'to enter into a stage of profound prayer and great silence, until some signs would confirm the message.'
"And the signs progressed. In March 1986, someone already offered me a house. Slavko, who came to Verona, encouraged me to seize this opportunity for the foundation. But two difficulties opposed one another:
    —How to bring together, in the same religious communnity, both men and women. And how to bring together the components of the traditional

celibate life, and the beginning for people who are married. And how to found that based on Medjugorje, since the Church had not approved these apparitions. Even here, the signs for the question asked, came at the meeting. In April 1986, I was invited to the International Assembly of the Renewal of the Spirit at Rimini. There I met Brothers and Sisters from the Community of 'Lion of Juda,' and from the 'Lamb Sacrificed' (Cordes, France), in white tunics and sandals, men, women and children. Some Brothers or Sisters were celibate, others married, all belonging entirely to this Community. I discovered the new Code of Canon Law (Canons 298 and 299) recognized for the laity and the clergy, the right to unite in private associations of the faithful, in order to lead a consecrated life. On June 6, in the course of an apparition, Maria received another message where Our Lady urged me to follow up the enterprise. At the same time, the requests were pouring in from many boys and girls whom the Madonna had chosen, oriented and gathered at random from retreats, letters, or telephone calls. The movement was becoming larger: two, then 10, then 20.

"On September 9th, Cardinal Ratzinger granted me an audience. I submitted to him two problems enroute to a solution: a community of men and women, celibate or married, founded on these apparitions. The Cardinal looked at me joyfully and said to me with a smile:

—'Why are you worried about it? Medjugorje—I'll take care of it. With respect to you, keep very well in mind a very important principle. It is necessary to distinguish between the facts which are in the course of investigation, and the fruits. It is up to *you* to think about them.

I invite you to much discernment in the vocations, and in the sustained contact with your bishop and your provincial. But, "go ahead." He stated to me precisely the formula of private association of the faithful, provided by the new Code of Canon Law.'

"On the following day, September 10th, I obtained unexpectedly, an audience with the Holy Father. I summarized for him the essential, and the Pope anticipated my question in relation to this foundation with Medjugorje. He said:

'But, Father, what are you concerned about? This problem with Medjugorje, my services are concerned with it. Concern yourself with vocations and move ahead.'

"He spoke to me with emotion. He embraced me as he said:

'The Madonna will open all the ways.'

"And as he gave me his rosary he said to me:

'Pray also, for me.'

"Thus, the way was opened. I left the audience on September 10th at one o'clock in the afternoon, and at the General Curie of the Passionists, I found a note:

'I will wait for you at Vicenza to see a house.'

"As early as the next day, I was at Priabona and visited this house where we presently are, and where the foundation began."

It is located in the Diocese of Vincenza, at the summit of an "inspired hill," with a sanctuary, and surrounded by some buildings. The utopian project, "Mary, Oasis of Peace," settled in this place quickly and without problems. The Passionist Provincial of Gianni Sgreva obtained, on September 20, 1986, an audience with Cardinal Ratzinger:

"It is a work of God," he confirmed.

The Superior General of the Passionists, impressed in turn, concluded:

"It is an honor for the entire congregation to welcome this new initiative where so many vocations meet."

On the 22nd of March, 1987, he signed the official approval. The Bishop of Vicenza, on which Priabona depends, did likewise on the 18th of May, 1987. On March 25th, 1987, the Feast of the Annunciation, the first members of the community made a day of retreat and signed "the private agreement" required by the Code of Canon Law for the approval of a private association of faithful (of which we give extracts in a note at the end of this chapter, on page 69). Many other candidates already gathered around the Oasis of Priabona.

The first candidates were all celibate. The project remained open to also welcome families. Father Sgreva concluded:

> "Everything rested on the gift of conversion which Mary multiplied at Medjugorje, and which led to the peace of God. The community wanted to express its 'solicitude for all men,' according to the formula of Redemptoris Mater (Mother of the Redeemer). It wants to realize in our unsacred, secularized, materialistic world, the recognition of the presence of God, who extends profound peace. As its name signifies, the community wants to be bearer of the Peace of God."

Gianni Sgreva then characterizes the community by three charisms:

1. INTERCESSION, which will be the object of a fourth vow, added to the traditional vows of poverty, chastity, obedience.
2. EXPIATION, because Our Lady cries in her own expiation, for sufferings of humanity plunged in sin. She suffers like a mother from this situation of the contemporary world, which cultivates alienation in reference to God with all its consequences. Therefore, let us not leave the Lord Jesus

all alone at Gethsemane. Let us not leave the Blessed Virgin all alone in her meditation as expiator.

3. RECEPTION of so many brothers and sisters in search of peace and a solution to their human problems, because faith is not locked up in intimacy, but must transfigure all of one's life.

The community will follow this project according to the purely contemplative vocation, and indicated by Our Lady. We will not produce any publicity. The community will move in the current of the inspiration which has founded it.

Priority of intercession has imposed, as evidence, that seven hours would be devoted to prayer, (six hours in community, plus one hour of personal prayer before the Holy Eucharist), organized progressively into perpetual adoration.

A day of adoration was formed on July 1st, 1987, all night adoration on October 1st ("Eco," #47, pg. 3).

"Seven hours—that seems considerable, greater than that provided by other fervent communities. Isn't that tempting Heaven and risking losing ground as it happens through excess of fervor?" I asked Gianni Sgreva at the time of my visit to Priabona.

"Experience has confirmed to us, during the first two months, that the Madonna requested that from us, and that our essential task is prayer. The reception for brothers and sisters will also call for effort and fatigue. The important thing is to pray with the heart."

One recognizes there another experience of Medjugorje.

"And the work?" I asked him again.

"For the time being, certainly, there is the arrangement and upkeep of the house, putting things in order, daily cooking and the rest, a little ground to cultivate. Will we do other work like earning a living? We already have some plans with respect to that. One will see in good time, according· to the principle of the Gospel:

Seek first the kingdom of God, and everything else will be given to you."

'And the direction of the community?'

"Well, it is Our Lady. Yes, it is really she. In our community meetings, an empty seat reminds us of her presence, at table, an (empty) plate for her. At the beginning of each Mass we invoke her so that she will help us enter into this mystery. In all our activities, we ask her to inspire us and to guide us. She is the Superior. We will live from her presence. It is she whom the bishop has designated as responsible for the community. . .

'You yourself?'

"Must be only an instrument in her hands. Let us hope that it will always be so.

'And the schedule?'

"It is similar to that of a classic community: at five o'clock, rising.

"At 5:30: Office of the readings (50 minutes), according to the monastic breviary of the Benedictins.

"At 6:30: Laudes.

"At 7:00: Mass (except Saturday and Sunday when the day follows the schedule of Medjugorje).

"At 8:30: Breakfast.

"Then a time of recollection, of study, or of catechism very necessary for many young vocations, which have never had catechism. And for the more advanced, theology (many began in October 1987).

"At 12:00 Noon: The Angelus, and the first chapelet of the rosary: The Joyful Mysteries.

"At 12:35: Lunch. But on Wednesdays, Fridays, and the vigils of feasts, according to the request of Our Lady at Medjugorje, there will be fasting on bread and water. There follows some time for recreation during which one sets in order the dining room and the kitchen.

"At 2:00 P.M.: Return to silence and eventual siesta, for whomever has not slept enough.

"At 3:00 P.M.: Knowns, followed by the second chapelet of the Rosary: The Sorrowful Mysteries and spiritual reading in common.

"Then two hours of work, recollection, catechism or music, as in the morning.

"At 6:00 P.M.: Vespers followed by a spontaneous prayer of praise or silence, or prayer for the healing. One will vary each day.

"At 7:30 P.M.: Dinner, followed by three-quarters of an hour of recreation and setting the house in order.

"At 8:45 P.M.: The third chapelet of the Rosary: The Glorious Mysteries.

"At 9:30 P.M.: Rest.

"The major part of the day is governed by silence. Not a disciplinary silence. The rule is that one speaks in order to cultivate the climate of prayer and of peace. It is in the same spirit that the meals are eaten in silence, but often with reading or listening to a cassette, and on certain feasts or during the last minutes, free conversation."

"With regard to the weekly tempo:
—On Monday evening: Two hours of prayer are foreseen before the Blessed Sacrament on the Mountain of the Cross from 9:00 to 11:00 p.m., strictly reserved for the members of the community.
—On Friday: One hour of prayer before the cross, to which the guests may be invited.
—On Saturday and Sunday: The afternoon prayers will unfold according to the daily model of Medjugorje. At the end of the morning, after the hours of Knowns, one will recite the first two

mysteries of the Rosary, then vespers, then the
Mass, prayer of healing, followed by the third
Mystery.

"You can see the convergence of harmony pre-
established between the parish life of Medjugorje
and the new monastic community of the Oasis.

"This community life allows for time for exchange.
Each Monday evening will be a sharing of fraternal
correction, which can eventually be extended into
the following day if something new requires it."

'Does community life of men and women, celibate for the most part, pose any problems?'

"In this climate, no. Our Lady, who once renewed
the image of the primitive Church, protects our
men/women relations from all sorts of confusion. The
involvement in the same objective induces the sur-
passing of problems or 'temptations,' if one wishes
to call them so. The climate of prayer and fraternal
communion takes care of the rest. Whoever might
be led toward such inclinations must tell the person
responsible; that will have, as an ordinary effect, to
free him from it. But the true source of the purity
of the relations is the Eucharist, which is at the center of community life. On July 6, 1987, we received
the decree which permits us to keep the Eucharistic
presence. It was the Feast of St. Maria Goretti, a
small sign which conveys the same meaning."

"On November 21, 1987, Feast of the Presentation of Our Lady, was the day of the first 13 investi-
tures, a great stage of development. The community
now numbers 22 members. It was a feast. The
brothers and the friends had decorated the house,
the church, and the statue of Our Lady in a most
beautiful way. Receiving the habit were five men
and eight women from very different areas and

professions. Barnaba came from Prague (Czecho-slovakia); Mary-Madeleine from Germany. With regard to the professions: Anna-Maria was professor of letters and philosophy at Modene; Lucie, a nurse; Marc, a student in physics at the University of Berlin; Maria-Fabrizia and Maria-Giovanni, workers; Paolo, a confectioner specialized in sugar icing; Tiziano, a geometrician. Many came from prayer groups in Medjugorje which are increasing in Italy.

"The 13 received the tunic (saio), grey-blue in color (the color of the apparition) with a maroon cincture from where a Rosary hung ('Our weapon!' said one at Priabona), and a cross on the chest. In addition, the Sisters received a white veil. These vestments, whose color was chosen by Maria Pavlovic, were blessed with the inspirations from Ephesians 6, the Biblical text on which the community was founded.

"The investiture was followed by the kiss of peace, whereupon 13 white doves flew off from the sacristy. It was the unexpected initiative of a brother. They seemed to find pleasure in remaining gathered at the feet of the statue of Our Lady, and remained there until the end of the office. The office ended with the entry into the community, of a couple, Giuseppe and Rita, with their 3 year old daughter."

On February 18, 1988, the community celebrated 9 months of existence. On March 25, the feast of the Annunciation, 7 brothers and sisters took the habit, among whom were Rita and Giuseppe (the married couple).

Three bishops visisted the community: Monsignor Hnilica, a Czech (July 6-7, 1987), Angelo Rivato (Brazil, January 5th and 16th), and Frane Franic, Archbishop of Split (February 14-15). While there, they shared the life and the exercises of the community, in a profound adherence to their extraordinary, spiritual, vitality.

Since that time, the community has undergone a new test.

The new bishop of the area (Vicenza), apprehensive of this new community, closed the church which his predecessor had given to them. The community tried to move to a monastery which a neighboring bishop had suggested, seeing the surge of vocations, and which now no longer took place at Priabona. But episcopal solidarity prevented this solution.

The community of Tomislav Vlasic is also undergoing the test. Tomislav had announced its foundation, along with a request for assistance, through a letter of March 25, 1988. He had believed he was able to proceed and with support from the seer Maria (April, 1988). But she left the community on July 5th to return to Medjugorje, and on July 11th her friends disseminated a correction, in which she declared not to have received from the Gospa, any approval of the community. She was also in disagreement with the alleged messages of Agnes Heupel (cured in Medjugorje), who had been chosen to guide the community. Too much zeal for Medjugorje aggravated these tensions, not without calumnies against Tomislav Vlasic. In August, Maria returned to Medjugorje. Tomislav Vlasic and his community made two trips to Medjugorje: end of July, and August 22nd. Three other members of the community of 14, remained at Medjugorje, while they remain affiliated with the community.

The new Provincial of the Franciscans, Jozo Vasilj, who took office in July, devoted himself to resolving the problems of this community which has essentially been formed from the prayer groups at Medjugorje. It seemed desirable that it settle at Medjugorje itself, without identifying with the fundamental fact of the apparitions which inspired so many legitimate and productive initiatives.

PLAN OF LIFE
MARY, OASIS OF PEACE

(May 18, 1987)

Here are some extracts of the plan of life (in 20 articles), signed by the first nine members of the community and approved by the General of the Passionist Fathers and by the

Bishop of Vicenza, on May 18, 1987. The preliminary text is Ephesians 6: 6-18, the Biblical inspiration of this founding text.

> *Put on the strength of the Lord and the armor of God to resist temptations...because our struggle is not against the creatures of flesh and blood, but against...the powers of darkness of this world. Be strong then, girded with the truth...the shield of the faith in hand, and the sword of the Spirit; that is to say: the Word of God.*
>
> *Pray unceasingly in vigilance and perseverance.* (*Eph.* 6: 10-18).

Imbued with these words, we note briefly what the Lord, through His mother, presents to our children-hearts: A simple outline where our agreement with God's plan shines forth:

1. We are grateful to the Blessed Virgin, Queen of Peace, because her maternal love has found us in our lives, and has made us find Jesus, the Lord, Prince of Peace. (*Is.* 9:5; *Eph.* 2:14).

2. The meeting with Mary has changed our lives...Now she invites us and educates us "with all kinds of prayers and supplications in the Spirit," and the love for penance and mortification, toward sanctity of a life which has been especially consecrated.

3. The abandonment to her, who, near the cross of Christ, became...the mother of humanity, requires our collaboration in order to save so many brothers and sisters in search of peace. We do not want to live egotistically only for ourselves, the gift which we have received...but be instruments in order to accomplish the plan of salvation of the Father.

4. With Mary, we have to help the return of humanity to God and the spiritual renewal of the Church. Since the Church was born in the school of prayer of Mary, we welcome the invitation of the Mother of the Church to return with her to the Cenacle, in order to learn from her, and with

her, the profoundness of prayer in the Spirit.

5. As in the primitive Cenacle with the apostles, there were men and women disciples, an integral Church in its first steps. Thus today, the Queen of Peace re-opens the school of the Cenacle with all the children of the Church: laity and clergy, men and women, celibate and married, with brothers chosen for the ordained ministry. Thus a new Pentecost is being prepared.

6. Through Mary, we have found peace again...through the consecration and the development of our contemplative community, true oasis of peace..., we want to be a private association of faithful, vowed to the ministry of intercession for the Church and all humanity, in order to ask for the gift of peace. (*Eph.* 6:18).

The plan of life later gives precise details on the ministry of intercession, the contemplative life, and the invitation to silence. It ends on rather austere dimensions:

11. Mary invites us to live a poor and restrained life on the personal, as well as community plan. Our economic resources are confidence and abandonment to Divine Providence, certain that if we live in faith and prayer, engaged in the Gospel and peace, and working with our hands, the Lord will not allow us to lack what is necessary, and will give us whatever to share His gifts with the poor. We will do nothing to pay the brothers, our hosts, and we do not desire to become owners of any real estate, according to the model of the primitive community and of the Gospel. (*Acts* 2: 42-46) and (*Mt.* 6: 24-26). The families and married couples will follow the economic rules, which will be established later on, on the basis of experience.

12. We want to love penance, mortification, interior and exterior fasting, as an indispensable demand for the ministry of intercession and expiation, because he is from the ancestory of demons that one drives away only through prayer and fasting... (*Mt.* 17:21).

Chapter 6

TESTIMONIES

Conversions and profound experiences continue at Medjugorje. They are innumerable. Here are some samples at random from mail which we have received (respecting the anonymity as in the preceding section).

A first testimony comes to us from the community of the Oasis, the community at Priabona:

"On August 11, 1987, at the hour of vespers, a young man about 20 years old came to us. Having completed his military service he had obtained from his captain an extraordinary permission for the reason which he explained to us:

" 'I could not stay in the barracks during the first anniversary of my conversion. I came to celebrate it with you.'

"And with great joyfulness, happy as a child, he related to us his adventure in this manner:

'Until last year (August 11, 1986), my life was discotheque and women. I would change every evening. I would play cards and would drink without paying, because I would always get out of it and return home drunk. I did not think of God. I didn't pray, and I would answer "no" to the repeated invitations from fervent uncles who wanted to lead me to Medjugorje. I avoided the occasions which they offered me to listen, to speak about it.'

"But one vacation day, I left for Yugoslavia. I went there to visit on the beach without any desire for Medjugorje."

After a long account of his adventures and an accident on the way, devoid of accuracy, he was suddenly left with a great desire to go to Medjugorje. He continued:

71

"I asked where it was. But the people did not know or they gave me the wrong directions. I spoke to the police and asked where Ljubuski (neighboring city) was in order not to raise their suspicions. From there to Medjugorje the trip is short. I arrived in front of the church. It was at night. But my joy was great and in the bottom of my heart I said, 'Thank you!' No one knew how to direct me to Jelena's house where my uncles received her hospitality. The day after, August 12th, I attended Mass in Italian, at 11 o'clock. A force drove me to receive Holy Communion. If I had thought of all the evil that I had done, particularly to girls and to their parents, I would have understood that I was not in a state to receive Holy Communion without Confession. After the Mass I looked for a priest for a long time. Finally, one of them listened to me in the sacristy, and ever since, I have gone to Confession every day, I found much joy in it. And after that, I smelled a perfume of cyclamens. I prayed before the statue, and I smelled the perfume. On returning from Medjugorje, I began to listen to priests, (up to that time objects of my mockeries). A priest talked to me about sin for a long time. I learned what must be the true Christian relationship between men and women. Since August 11th, I no longer frequented discotheques nor looked at pornographic newspapers and films.

"My heart sings. When I look at the host during the elevation, I think:

'You, Jesus, have cured my heart.'

"I could have gone through the walls with joy. Now, for several months, I am here at the barracks. Poor buddies! (Many have parents in dissension; we know that one has a lover). They have their children aborted. They think they can find happiness and pleasure. Some of them participate in black masses and design crosses with dates of birth and of death. They distribute copies of a leaflet which invites people to swear faithfulness to Satan while denying Baptism. Many sign up; then they regret it. But oftentimes they take drugs, and something else in them is destroyed. Satan is a minister of death.

"Many of our officers are evil and do not know what else to invent to harm us. They are in a great internal suffering. The first officer is all blasphemy. It had affected me in the worst way. Thank you, Lord, because it is no longer my problem. I have never been so happy as I am now. Jesus loves us. I attend a prayer group outside of the camp. Twelve months of military service is an inhuman, insurmountable test. In the month of May 1986 [before the conversion] I had fallen into a depressive crisis. It is by faith that I got out of it, while going to daily Mass and going to Confession. And then Mary helped me. Thanks to Jesus, I have been the instrument of conversion for some youngsters, but very few. I try to speak about Jesus and to help everyone. Some say to me:

'What must I do in order to be happy like you?'

"Go to Confession."

"But everyone cites examples to me of priests who are not good. Yes, some priests are not good, but I tell them:

"If one host falls to the ground, you do not trample on it! We should not speak ill of priests, but pray for them. And one must be attentive in choosing a priest who is good. Yes, in every youth, there is something good. But you must wait for and ask the Lord to give you the right words to touch hearts.

"Today I went to pray with my parents and to pray the stations of the cross with them. I am happy, overflowing with joy. One year ago, I began this path of faith. I wish it for everyone." (Priabona, August 11, 1987).

The "Eco" of October 1987 (No. 45) cited another testimony. It concerns a young girl, twenty-two years of age, a sweet face, which is today all smiles, but hides a sad story:

"God threw me from my horse on the road to Damascas. I had never been a good girl. My life experiences became submerged in sin. Educated harshly by my father, at the age of 17, I gave myself to his associate and I had a first abortion. At 18, I left home to work in Milan, in fashions. And there, being a 'beautiful girl,' I entered the circle of rich people. I became familiar with the milieu which permitted me to become well-known, someone in television and in the newspapers. I began to live among the richest in Italy, but the scarcity of work, because of the competition and the need for money, drove me to ask my father for money. His only response was:

'If you want to be better, you must return home.'

"I answered 'No.'

"This same malignant fever grew inside of me. The need for money led me to meet a multimillionaire. Since he was already married to someone else, I became his mistress and gave myself over to all his desires in order to be independent of my father. It is there that I found happiness. A friend helped me to enter a circle of multimillionaires in Europe. I began to prostitute myself with a man, who at first was sweet, but then determined to exploit me. I began telling myself: 'When I acquire a little more money, I will leave.' But, the more I earned, the more I spent and the more I needed, and I was forced to maintain these bonds at a high financial level. I was admired. People treated me well. But I was always miserable because, being sensitive, I had a thirst for affection in this bleak environment. I had recourse to cocaine and alcohol until the age of 19. I spent the nights with very rich men, always more given to prostitution. I would wake up at one or two in the afternoon, stuffed with sleeping pills. I would continue to drink, not finding any love, but only cruelty around me. I destroyed all that was human in me and would pervert the girls who associated with me. Thus, 19-1/2 years of life, and mine was only sadness. It was then that I met the multimillionaire with whom I had been with, up until the last two months. Consequently, I stopped prostituting myself, but, in spite of this man, I still spent the nights with two or three wealthy men who paid me back with gifts, jewels, clothes. Each time I freed myself from it, there flowed in me a destruction, psychic and physical at the same time, and I overcame despair only in drinking. During this last year, I also had four true loves. But one after the other, the relationship quickly ended and that left me sad, disillusioned, battered, to the point of trying several times to commit suicide. I thought, 'God has loved me since he has permitted me to get out of prostitution.'

"I looked for a way to change my millionaire friend, who was a little crazy. I often consulted fortune-tellers and card readers in order to discover what life had in store for me because, deep down, I still dreamt of meeting an honest man, marrying him, having five of six children, and living in the country. There was a young girl, a close friend of mine, who, although she was in the same predicament as I, was so very kind to me. But, I treated her badly. I had become a real animal.

"Altogether, for three years, my life was possessed by the devil. I existed no more. I loved sex, money, and I lived in orgy and on drugs. I had everything; more than a young girl could dream of. I was able to satisfy every desire, but indeed my life was empty and dead. I seemed the most fortunate, but I was the most desperate. In the eyes of others, I was brilliant. I had succeeded. But really, everything appeared to me to be artificial; I was burned out and unhappy. Is this the way that the world destroys its adorers?"

"Twenty-one years! For a year I had begun to experience the call of Medjugorje. A mother was calling me. A television documentary struck me. I said to myself; 'When will the day arrive for me, also?' In a book purchased at the train station, I found three or four prayers of Medjugorje, and I experienced a stronger need to recite them, even when I returned home at two or three in the morning. Then, four months ago, I argued with my man, then with another, then with my best friend. But I felt that something had changed in me. In May, I had a phone conversation with my sister, who was somewhat crazy, and for whom I had prayed to Saint Rita. After going to Medjugorje, she returned from there completely cured. She insisted: 'Go to Medjugorje!'

"But a voice within kept repeating: 'It is not yet your time.' I had convinced a dear person who lived in my style to go to Medjugorje. First, she laughed at me, then she went there. When she returned she seemed to me an angel. She prayed, she cried, she loved God, and she became detached from all amusement. I felt that my time had come. I began to fast once a week. But so many obstacles got in the way of my going. I almost didn't find a place on the plane. I was seized with the doubt of 'the aftermath.' How will I detach myself from my habits? The night before leaving I went out with friends and committed, I think, the last grave sins. Finally, I left, and in Split I met a group of beautiful young people. I arrived at Medjugorje at night. I stayed there two days without eating, without sleeping, because I seemed to have no more interest in those things.

"On the morning of July 25, 1987, I do not recall the exact moment, I began to enter into an ecstasy of spirit and heart. God was very near. In those 20 minutes, God gave me the grace to experience His love. I was moved to think only about it. He made me see and experience His way. What I experienced then, I have not experienced any more since, but that was enough for me to be through with my previous life, and become really poor. I gave everything away, gold, money, and I remained without anything. To dress up, to adorn myself, to be beautiful, to have a good time, friends, the world—in a word, what I believed beautiful previously, suddenly left my life. That doesn't exist for me any more."

"In those 20 minutes, I experienced that my life must be only in Christ, for God, with the Madonna. She placed me in the hands of Father Jozo [in Thyalina], who heard my confession and made me feel the sweetness with which Jesus forgave me. A week later I returned to Medjugorje, to spend more time there. I can not express the graces that I received during those days, especially a great love for prayer, which became a real meeting with Jesus and His Mother. Little by little, the desire for a total consecration was born in me.

"On my return to Milan, it is Jesus who will henceforth guide me where He wishes. In comunities and prayer groups, I often experience Jesus and His life until I feel very badly. Without prayer, I would not be able to live any longer, even an hour. My love towards Jesus grows from day to day. I do not think of the future but I ask continuously to abandon myself to Him. The devil does not stop tempting me, in a very strong way—not to make me return to my former life, but with little things, (which are indeed great) in trying to keep me at a distance from my vocation. I sometimes spend two or three hours in doubt and in anguish. Should I marry, have children? But after praying, I experience a love so great that I tell myself 'No, neither children nor husband would be able to give me the same love.'" (Testimony of September 24, 1987).

Two months later, in December, she entered the community with her sister, and sent a long testimony, signed Dalila.

"Now I understand that it is I who wanted all the faults committed in my life. I was able to choose because God leaves us free. But very often I am disillusioned with the false light of a worldly society, where everything is only instant joy and happiness. Now has come the true sweetness (undoubtedly obtained through the continuous prayers of my mother). His love wanted to save His little flower, stained by the poisonous wind of the world, in giving it the salvation of the Resurrection. Today, day after day, His sweetness fills my heart more than did the alcohol, wealth, good times, and the great loves. In brief, all the consolations of the earth are only bitterness for me.

"All have disappeared because there can exist no love greater than that which my Jesus gives me now. Jesus is not a distant God, eager to judge me or to punish me for my immense faults and sins of each day; because such appear to be the smallest failures to one who loves. It is better to suffer a little in this life for the love of Jesus, than to enjoy a little and to be damned for eternity. I am in Him, in Jesus, His true peace, true happiness, true love which burns, but which does not consume." (signed: Dalila).

Still Dalila confessed:

"Accustomed to the easiness of worldly life, it is sometimes difficult for me to face the sacrifice of community life. When I have to get up for morning prayer, it seems to me that I am going through some torture, and yet I am happy. I want to consecrate myself and everything completely to my Jesus. Even if there are many ups and downs and little doubts, I separate myself from them because I know that they come from the evil one. I am certain that there is not a way more marvelous, than that on which the Lord has put me."

And here are a collection of testimonies from different locations:

"I went to Medjugorje for two weeks. It was really extraordinary. I returned completely changed." (Testimony from Spain).

"I had the grace to be present at an apparition in the presbytery. When Jakov, at the end of the ecstasy, said, 'Ode' (gone), I had the grace to understand and feel the light breath, the light wind of her presence, which was leaving us. That left me deeply emotional."

"The messages of Medjugorje have changed our lives, my husband and I. Conversion of the heart has been realized. We devote as much time as possible to the recitation of the Rosary, we fast twice a week and attend Mass three or four times. We visit the Blessed Sacrament often." (Testimony from Canada).

"We received in Medjugorje and since then, numerous important graces, of which was renewal of faith, of prayer, and daily Mass; and then the conversion of a son-in-law, and the return to the right path of one of our children. And each day there are so many small things, so good, to be discerned and to be savored." (Testimony from Morbihan).

"My wife and I went on a pilgrimage (five days) to Medjugorje, and we can certify that we received there, many corporal and spiritual graces. Corporal for myself, having been disabled in the course of a gall bladder operation, and after having surgery four different times, I was in a state of crisis before departure. After Medjugorje, nothing more. May thanks be given to Jesus and Mary.

"Spiritual for the two of us. Our faith and our practice of religion have been revived: fasting, Confession, prayer. A great thanks to Our Lady of Medjugorje." (Testimony of A and D. B.C., end of 1987).

"I received very much at Medjugorje, but I found an obstacle in the pastor of my parish. When I approached this subject, even before I am able to express myself, he responds to me: 'Medjugorje is forbidden. I refuse to discuss it further.'

"If I were the only one concerned it would not matter to me, for after four pilgrimages my conviction and the fruits remain. But these authorized warnings have a negative action on thousands of faithful. What can one do in peace?" (Testimony of G. of B. end of 1987).

"On September 14, 1987, someone led me to the hill of the apparitions between nine and 10 o'clock in the evening. I received there the grace of conversion and abandonment, with an immense joy on the path of return. I experienced, very strongly, the presence of the Blessed Virgin. On the day after, in the church, around me and in my heart, I had to catch myself in order not to fall." (Testimony of Seine-etMarne).

"I thought only of work and money, and my family suffered from my lack of affection. And then I went on a pilgrimage to Medjugorje. Among the crowd in prayer, I was distressed. The sermon was in Croatian, but I had the impression that it was being addressed only to me. On returning, I did not have any more money for the essentials and yet I was able to return without spending a penny. Now I believe; I pray with my family and I have understood the essential, life with God." (Testimony of Var).

"At Medjugorje, one thinks he is touching Heaven. That came to me three times. Yes, Jesus is truly the Son of God. He is truly the Son of Mary." (Testimony from Belgium).

"The reading of your books on Medjugorje has caused in me a profound inspiration to prayer and penance, and a great desire to go there." (G of B, Paris, November 16, 1987).

Medjugorje has suggested to scientist, Xavier Sallantin, a long, inspired analysis whose conclusion is as follows:

"Medjugorje constitutes a challenge for science. These events provide a new possibility to observe the inexplicable. That comes at a time when physicists are quite confronted, if not by the inexplicable in quantum physics, at least by a manner of communication among particles, which is not explained according to the traditional representation of the physical reality. That compels science to a reconsideration of a heartrending question of its materialism in principle. Thus, the absence of a new intelligibility, whose manifestation could have unimaginable consequences. It would contain on its way, scientific revelation and religious revelation, combined in the clarity of one and the same light, that of the glorious Christ, where the plan of love would become vivid evidence for all of mankind.

"It is important to underline this conceptual revolution because God would not know how to cheat creation. What we call supernatural actually manifests itself in the heart of the nature according to the arrangements which providence has made in creation, and which science has partially eliminated. It is to say that God has arranged what we call 'nature' so that prayer is efficacious, that perceptions called extra-sensorial (like those of the seers) be possible, that the miracles take place, that His grace be effective, that His plan of love be accomplished in the respect of our liberty, etc. We do not know how that works, but we do not have any reason to exclude it, in this story of salvation, whose stages are so authoritatively explained in *Redemptoris Mater*, (Mother of the Redeemer). We have access to the understanding of the admirable interaction between the natural and the supernatural, between the visible and the invisible, between the created and the unborn, in the image of the relationship of love among the Divine Persons. Then we will see face-to-face, then we will know as we are known.

"At Medjugorje, Mary does not cease to refer to her intervention in the realization of the Divine plan. It is a design which Paul says: *Formed in advance to be realized when the times will be accomplished, to bring back all things under one leader, Christ, the heavenly creatures and the earthly creatures.* (*Eph.* 1:10). Mary, in her holy, maternal, personal way, has been sent to us to rekindle the hope of such a gathering and perhaps to suggest the imminence of it." (X. Sallantin in *Association of Friends of Teilhard de Chardin*, May 1987, No. 126, p. 12).

Richard Foley, S.J. has published in *"Catholic Herald,"* November 22, 1985, an interview with the great theologian, Urs von Balthasar, from which emerged the following remarks:

"The concluding proof of the authenticity of Medjugorje is in the quantity and the quality of the fruits. The totally occasional contact with books, video, pilgrimages, causes some graces of peace, faith, profoundness, a desire to pray more, the courage to fast on bread and water, of regularly frequenting the sacraments. But beyond these spiritual graces, these apparitions warn us that this world is in danger. The Mother of God invites us to stave off the horror through prayer and fasting. This completely orthodox message nourishes in us, the respect for the Divine authority of the Church."

And here are the conclusions of Monsignor Paola Hnilica, Bishop of Czechoslovakia, resident in the Vatican, a close friend of Pope John Paul II, whom he informed on his return from his pilgrimages to Medjugorje:

"Approximately a hundred specialists have examined the phenomena of Medjugorje under their magnifying glass. Their conclusions are generally positive. Likewise, the conclusions of millions of pilgrims who have come to Medjugorje. How does one explain it? There are three possibilities: God, human capacity, or Satan.

1. The evil one is to be automatically excluded because it would be very astonishing for him to call people to conversation, reconciliation, to prayer, fasting, adoration of the Blessed Sacrament, and a devotion to Mary.
2. Man's capacities would not be able to explain all the phenomena. For example, none of the seers has a theological background to invent these evangelical messages.
3. Now, does one wish to verify that the phenomena comes from God? Jesus, Himself, gives us the criterion: *'You will recognize the tree by its fruits.'*

(*Matthew* 7:16). The fruits of Medjugorje are positive, very positive, complimentary to those of Lourdes and Fatima, including the frequent interior and physical cures." (P. Hnilica, extract of articles published in *Stella Maris, 1987).

BEFORE THE MIRACLE: Rita Klaus in April 1986.

AFTER THE MIRACLE: Christmas 1986.

Photos courtesy of Pittsburgh Center for Peace, Queen of Peace Newsletter.

Chapter 7

SOME OF THE LATEST MESSAGES

We will cite the latest ones because the interest which so many Christians express in the messages of Medjugorje, the fruits which they produce, have led me to collect them in a volume written in collaboration with Professor René Lejuene: *The Messages and Teachings of Mary at Medjugorje*.

Here, as a continuation, are some of the latest messages:

January 25, 1988

> *Dear children, even today I invite you to total conversion. It is difficult for all those who have not chosen God. It is in God that I invite you to total conversion, dear children. God can give you everything that you ask him, but you look for God only when illnesses, problems, and difficulties arise, and you think that God is far from you, that He does not listen to you, and does not answer your prayers.*
>
> *No, dear children, if you are far from God, you cannot receive graces, you do not ask for them with a strong faith. I pray for you from day-to-day. I wish to bring you closer to God, more and more, but I cannot if you do not want it. For that, dear children, put your life in the hands of God. I bless all of you."*

Since the beginning of February, the apparition at night on the hill, (toward 10 to 11 o'clock at night), around Ivan, Maria and sometimes Vicka, often gives a brief message:

Monday, February 1, 1988

Under a full moon and starlit sky, Ivan was there, Vicka also, but she did not have the apparition. Our Lady came with five angels. Ivan did not say that she was happy, as he usually says. She prayed for each one, recited the "Our Father" and "Glory Be," and gave this message:

> *Prepare yourselves for the season of Lent in giving up something in these 40 days. I need your help for the accomplishment of all my plans.*

Monday, February 8th

Ivan was absent (in Israel), and Vicka, who was present, did not see her on that day. Maria alone had the apparition of Our Lady, who was accompanied by angels. She gave this message:

> *I ask you to seriously commit yourselves to the path of holiness.*
> *Dear children, I want to help you.*

And joyfully, she ascended into Heaven.

Monday, February 22nd (the same place)

Maria transmitted this message.

> *Dear children, I am happy for you, for your self-denials during this Lenten season, but I am particularly appreciative for your giving up sin. Encourage others toward conversion, peace, a change of life. Let your light shine. Give very much love to others. Show them love.*

After having prayed with them the "Our Father" and the "Glory Be," she went away with a sign of a shining cross as she said: *Go in the peace of God..*

February 29th

> *Dear children, abandon all your problems and difficulties to Jesus and pray. Pray, pray, pray. During this month, every evening, pray before the cross in thanksgiving, that until the death of Jesus.*

March 7th

> *I am your Mother and I warn you that Satan wants to destroy everything that we have begun. That is why pray very much.*

March 14th

> *Dear children, Satan, during this period of Lent, wants by every means possible to destroy in you everything that we have begun. I forewarn you insofar as I am your Mother. May prayer be a weapon against him.*

March 21st

Dear children, today, also, your Mother wants to forewarn you that Satan is seeking with all the means possible, to destroy everything in you. But your prayer does not permit him to suceed. With your prayers you fill up the voids and in this manner, you prevent Satan from entering into your soul. Pray, dear children, and your Mother will pray with you in order to conquer Satan. Let this time be one in which all of us give ourselves and share our peace with others. Then, if you wish, share your peace with others. Then, if you want, share peace with your families, on the streets, everywhere. I am happy because your prayer is strong and persistent.

March 25th (the monthly message sent from Italy by Maria):

Dear children, even today I call you to complete abandonment to God. Dear children, you are not conscious of the love with which God loves you. That is why He permits me to be with you, to teach you, to help you, to find the road to peace. But you cannot find that road if you do not pray. That is why, dear children, leave everything and devote your time to God and He will give you then gifts, He will bless you.

Little children, do not forget that your life is fleeting as are the flowers in the spring, which today are beautiful, but which tomorrow, no one will think of. That is why, pray, so that your prayer and your abandonment to God be as a guide on your route, thus your testimony will have value not only for you, but for all eternity.

March 28th

Pray as much as possible before Easter. Pray this week every day two hours, before the cross.

Easter Monday, April 4th

Give love and joy to others. Pray for peace.

April 11th

Dear children, I am your Mother and I ask you to be converted. Pray particularly for those who blaspheme.

April 25th

Message for the parish:

Dear children, God wants to make you holy. Through me, He is inviting you to complete surrender. Let Holy Mass be your life. Understand that the Church is God's palace, the place in which I gather you and want to show you the way to God. Come and pray! Neither look at others, nor slander them. Rather let your life be a testimony on the way of holiness. Churches deserve respect and are set apart as holy because God, who became man, dwells in them day and night.

Little children, believe and pray that the Father will increase your faith; then you can ask for whatever you need. I am with you and I am rejoicing because of your conversion; and I am protecting you with my motherly mantle. Thank you for your response to my call.

Monday, May 9th (on Krizevac)

Let this month be one of praying the Rosary and reading the Bible. Satan wants to destroy your plans.

Monday, June 6th (on Podbrodo, after 10:00 P.M.)

Dear children! I have been coming here for seven years. I ask you to relive the messages which I give you. These are messages of prayer, of peace, of fasting and of sacrifice. Make sacrifices yourselves. All the other messages flow from these fundamental messages. Thank you for responding to my call. I am your Mother. Open your hearts to this grace.

Monday, August 1st

I am asking you to pray very much before Friday. Live this Friday in joy. I am asking you also to pray this evening as you return to your homes, the Glorious Mysteries of the Rosary, before the cross. (Ivan reminded all that this Friday, August 5th is the birthday of Mary, according to the messages received at Medjugorje in 1985).

Thursday, August 4th (on Podbrodo at midnight the Blessed Virgin appeared in radiance, dressed in gold).

My dear children! My Son has sent me among you this evening. I am happy with you. I am happy to see you in such large numbers. I wish for this joy to remain all day. Live this joy in prayer. Live in the joy. I give you my love so that love may be your life. Make love grow around you. Your Mother loves you. I am happy this evening. Yet, I need your help. I wish to work with you and I need your cooperation. I am not able to do anything without you.

Monday, August 8th (on Podbrodo at 11:00 P.M.)

Your Mother asks you to pray for young people in the world. Remember them in prayer before the feastday.

Friday, August 12th (on Krizevac)

Dear children! Your Mother wishes you to pray as much as you can during these 2 days. Prepare yourselves in prayer for the feastday. In these days carry peace to others. Encourage others to change. You are not able to extend peace around you if you yourselves do not have peace within. This evening, I give peace. Give it to others.

Monday, August 15th (Feast of the Assumption, at 11 P.M., Ivan and Maria—who had returned from Italy—see Our Lady on Podbrodo. She wore a dress of gold and her joy was limitless).

Dear children! Beginning today, begin a new year, a year for the youth. During this year, pray for the young, speak to young people. They are now in a very difficult situation. Help them and one another. I think of you in a special way dear children. Young people have a role to play now, in the Church. Pray dear children.

After this, there was an interruption of the messages on the hill until mid-October.

ADDITIONAL MONTHLY MESSAGES
(Given by Maria the 25th of the month)
July 25th, 1988

Today I invite you to a complete abandonment to God. Everything that you do and everything that you possess, give it to God so that He may reign over your life as King, over everything which you possess. Thus, through me, God will be able to lead you to the total depth of the spiritual life.

Do not be afraid because I am with you even when you think there is no longer any solution and that Satan is at work here. I bring you peace. I am your Mother and The Queen of Peace. I bless you with the blessing of joy. Let God be everything in your life.

August 25th

Today I invite all of you to rejoice in the life which God gives you. Dear children, rejoice because of God the Creator, who has so marvelously created you. Pray so that your life will be a joyful praise, like a river, so that it will flow from your heart.

Dear children, give thanks unceasingly for everything that you have, even for the least gifts which God has given you. Thus, God will always pour out on your life, a blessing which overflows with joy.

September 25th

I invite all of you, without exception, to the path of holiness in your life. God has provided you a gift of holiness. Pray, so that you may know it better. Thus you will be able to give testimony to God by your life.

Dear children, I bless you and intercede for you, close to God, so that your path and your testimony be complete and be a joy for God.

APPENDICES AND DOCUMENTS

Number 1

Monsignor Pavao Zanic's Homily, July 25, 1987, at Medjugorje.

(at the time of the confirmation of 130 young children on the Feast of St. James, Patron Saint of the Parish—Mentioned above pages 7 to 20).

Brothers and Sisters,

Here I am today in Medjugorje for the Confirmation. You are hoping, perhaps, that I tell you some words on these events about which everybody is speaking. The Church must take them upon herself, and that is why, in the interest of all, she confides the inquiry to special commissions. You know that it is currently in discussion in the commission formed by the Episcopal Conference in Yugoslavia because the Church cannot so easily involve its authenticity, facing the world of the Twentieth Century. It is only trying to criticize it in saying "Since you are in error, who is this Jesus Christ to whom you belong?"

Already after six years, I can tell you. I have prayed, examined and kept silent. Many others have prayed and I thank them. At each Mass I had an intention for Medjugorje. In each Rosary every day I prayed to the Blessed Virgin to obtain for me from God and the Holy Spirit, the light. Thus, I acquired a solid conviction founded on all that I heard, read, and lived.

Here, one prays very much and one fasts, but all that on the conviction that these events are truly supernatural. To preach to the blessed people of the faithful the lie about God, Jesus, and the Blessed Virgin deserves the bottom of Hell.

In all my investigations, prayers, or inquiries, I had only one goal: to arrive at the truth. In this regard I had formed, since 1982, a commission of four members. Later, with the aid of some bishops and religious provincials, I increased it to 15 members. These members were professors of theology representing seven dioceses and four provinces, likewise two psychiatrists of great renown, who had the freedom of consulting their colleagues. The commission worked for three years and during this period the public was informed about its work through its communication. Currently, this problem is treated by the Commission already mentioned, formed by the Episcopal Yugoslav Conference. Indeed, those who were pressed, have preceded the judgment of the Church, have proclaimed miracles and have spoken of supernatural events in preaching from the pulpit on private revelations. That is not permitted before the Church has authenticated these revelations.

That is why different requests have been made not to organize pilgrimages, but to wait for the judgment of the Church. Since March 24, 1984, the commission for Medjugorje sent out a directive on this matter. Unfortunately, without results. In the month of October of this same year, the Episcopal Yugoslav Conference repeated the request not to organize any official pilgrimages to Medjugorje. By "official," one understands every pilgrimage organized in a group. That did not help any.

That is why the Congregation for the Doctrine of the Faith in Rome, sent, on May 23rd, 1985, a letter to the Episcopal Conference of Italy[1] to ask the Italian bishops to restrain the organization of pilgrimages as well as every propaganda on this matter. But it remained without any results. Finally, when the commission was formed at the level of the Episcopal Conference, his eminence, Cardinal Kuharic and the Bishop of Mostar, sent, in the name of the Episcopal Conference of Yugoslavia on January 9th, 1987, a memorandum which stated: "It is likewise forbidden to organize pilgrimages and other manifestations which would be motivated by the supernatural character attributed to the facts of Medjugorje." This was said at the highest level in the Church[2] and one cannot proceed further as if it were nothing. (See footnotes on page 131).

After the first news on the events in this parish, the Ordinary [Monsignor Zanic] followed them attentively and gathered all he could to serve the investigation of the truth. The bishop permitted the seers and the priests of the parish complete freedom. He even defended them from the attacks of the press and the political authorities [in August, September, 1981]. All the interviews were recorded on cassettes. We gathered chronicles and diaries, letters and documents, and all that was studied by professors of theology and doctors. The final result of this commission has been the following: two members of the commission judged the apparition supernatural and authentic, and voted for it. A member abstained, and another one believed that the apparitions were only true at the beginning. The eleven others concluded that there were no apparitions.

I am deeply convinced that all of the members of the Commission worked conscientiously and researched the truth, in the documents which they had at hand. The Church cannot risk its authenticity. That is why, very often, in similar cases she examined closely all the events and forbade the crowds to gather in these places until it was established that the events were not supernatural. Let us remember Garabandal in Spain, San Damiano in Italy, and some ten other similar places known in our days. At Garabandal, the seers said that the Blessed Virgin had promised a great sign for the whole world. Twenty-five years passed since, and the great sign has not taken place. If the Blessed Virgin had left here a sign, it would have cleared for everyone, and we would know what it was about.

When the Blessed Virgin began to appear at Podbrdo, on Crnica hill, the police forbade access to it. Then, this Virgin moved about into the homes, enclosures, in the fields, in the vineyards, in tobacco fields. She appeared in the church on the altar, in the Sacristy, in the choir, under the roof, on the belfry, on the road, on the route to Cerno, in the car, in the bus, at school, in Mostar and Sarajevo, in different places, in Zagreb, in the convents, in Varazdin, in Switzerland, in Italy, and again in Podbrdo, on Krizevac, in the parish, in the rectory, etc. I have not named half of the places of these alleged apparitions. Consequently a clear thinking man, who honors the Blessed Virgin, asks himself, "Our Lady, what are they doing with you?"

In this diocese, I am, by divine right, pastor, master of the Faith, and judge on these questions. Since it has been established that events in Medjugorje have created the tension and division in the Church (some believe, others do not believe), that they are escaping from the control of the Church, and because the decisions and recommendations of the requests already mentioned, (the Commission, the Congregation and the Episcopal Conference), have remained without effect: I, Bishop of Mostar, responsible before God for the discipline in my diocese, repeat and confirm the preceding decision of ecclesiastical request; and, the priests who organize pilgrimages and come here attributing to these events a supernatural character before the work of the Episcopal Conference has been concluded, are forbidden the celebration of Mass.

I address you, Immaculate Virgin, Mother of God, and Mother of the Church, Mother of this faithful people who look to you, who pray to you and love you, I address you, Me, your servant, the Bishop of Mostar, and, before the whole world, I express my profound and unshakable faith in all the privileges with which God has presented you, and through which you are the first and the most perfect creature. I express my profound and unshakable faith in your protection and intercession before God, all Powerful, for all the needs of your children in this valley of tears. I express my profound and unshakable faith in your love for us sinners. This love you have proved by your help and your apparitions. I, myself, guided pilgrimages to Lourdes.

And, precisely, due to the strength of this faith, I, your servant, Bishop of Mostar, before this assembly and this crowd, which invoked you, I reveal and I recognize your great sign, which has become for me sure and clear after six years. I do not need a spiritual sign, but those who believe in the lie, needed one. "This sign is your silence" persistent in spite of so many announcements of a great sign: "It is going to be given on Apparition Hill, visible and permanent, soon, very soon. A little longer. Be patient!" They said all of that in 1981. Then: it is going to take place at such and such a feast—on Christmas, on New Years.

I thank you, Our Lady, for having shown by your silence for six years that you did not speak here, that you did not appear, and that you have not given messages nor secrets, and that you did not promise a particular sign.

Very Blessed Virgin, Mother of Christ, our Mother, intercede for the peace in the diocese of Mostar where the Church is troubled. Intercede more particularly in this place, for this parish, where innumerable times your Holy Name has been used for words which were not of you. Give us the grace so that one can cease inventing these messages. Receive, Most Holy Virgin, in reparation, the sincere prayers of pious souls who are far from being fanatic. . .and from having a disobeying heart. Help us all to arrive at just truth. Dear Gospa, amiable and obedient servant of the Lord, we pray to you so that Medjugorje may start off on a sure step following the pastor of the local church so that all of us together can glorify you and praise you in the truth of love. Amen!

Number 2

INTERVIEW WITH VICKA

By A. Bonifacio with the aid of Sister Josipa, interpretor

WHY DISTRACTIONS IN OUR PRAYERS?
August 5, 1987

Bonifacio: "What does the Gospa recommend?"

Vicka: "We must really change; begin to pray and then we will discover what she expects of us, where she wants to lead us. If one does not begin to pray and to open his heart, then we will not understand even what she expects of us."

Bonifacio: "The Gospa always says to pray well, with the heart, and pray only, but she does not willingly give prescriptions on how to learn to pray thus. Why am I always distracted?"

Vicka: "The desire of Our Lady is: *Pray only.* But before arriving at praying only, and really with the heart, it is necessary to start and, in order to begin, you open a space in your heart, in your person, for the Lord, trying to free yourself from all that troubles you and prevents this contact with prayer. And when you are thus free, you can begin to really pray with the heart, to say an 'Our Father.' You can say very little in prayers, but it is necessary to say them with the heart, and afterwards, little by little, when you say these prayers, all your words become really a part of your life. Then you are able to pray with joy."

Bonifacio: "Often, prayer does not enter into our lives because our times of prayer are separate from our action, and are not translated into our lives. There is a division. How do you get out of it?"

Vicka: "One must reach the point that prayer becomes really a joy for us, just like work becomes a joy. If, for example, you say, 'Now I give up praying because I have too much to do,' it is because you love work more than prayer. It might demand an effort on your part, but if you really love to meet the Lord, if you love to speak with Him, prayer becomes a joy from which will come forth your manner of being, of doing, of working."

Bonifacio: "How does one convince the skeptics, those who laugh at all that?"

Vicka: "It is not with words that you will convince. Don't even try it. It is your life, your love, your constant prayer for them which will convince them of the reality which you live." ("Eco," No. 45, October, 1987, Pg. 11).

Number 3

INTERVIEW WITH JELENA VASILIJ

By Nicoletta Valsecchi and Alberto Bonifacio
August 5, 1987

Question: "What has Our Lady told you during these last days?"

Jelena: "As always, to pray: In prayer, to feel God near. She invites us to thank God for everything. She says that prayer is like a light on our way. Then, if we pray, we can really understand what the Lord wants from us. Thus, He tells us to accept every cross, every difficulty because it is through the cross we will succeed in understanding the love of God. She invites us to see Jesus in everything; in every person; to love Him in everyone...through prayer."

Question: "Yesterday, did you receive any particular message?"

Jelena: "The Madonna only told me to thank God always for everything He has give us here, during these years." (of the apparitions).

Question: "Has this experience changed you?"

Jelena: "Yes, the Gospa has helped me very much to pray more, with more love, with more confidence in God. My spiritual life has really changed."

Question: "And what is the importance of fasting?"

Jelena: "The Gospa tells us that fasting helps us to grow in the spiritual life. Not only fasting on bread and water, but also fasting in so many things which give us pleasure. She tells us to do it with the heart...as a joy and not as a responsibility."

Question: "The Gospa speaks mortification, penance. What does that mean?"

Jelena: "It is important to be always on one's guard, more attentive to the way of God."

Question: "How does she want us to pray?"

Jelena: "She invites us especially to Holy Mass, then to the Rosary. She also says: every prayer is good, every prayer has value."

Question: "What does: 'To pray with the heart' mean, and how does one arrive at this prayer of the heart?"

Jelena: "Prayer of the heart is when we truly experience prayer, to be together with Jesus, to spend good moments with Him. It is when we do it, not by force or responsibility, but with the heart, to be with Jesus, to follow His way, to live the Gospel effectively."

Question: "Sometimes one prays, but the heart is somewhere else."

Jelena: "It is necessary to place oneself in the hands of the Lord, because it is not we who can change our heart. But we can trust it to the Lord and to pray, asking Him for His help."

Number 4

INTERVIEW WITH VICKA

By Sister Margherita Makarovic
September, 1987

"I was Vicka's guest in her house. I discovered her as a palpable sign of the presence of Mary, a witness to her love, an incarnation of her messages... For 20 days, she had to confine herself to bed with inflammation of the lungs and fever from 39 to 40 degrees "C." The doctors in Zagreb prescribed a cure for her. She did not want to take any remedy and did not agree to be isolated from visitors. Drug addicts had a free access to her home."

Question: "Vicka, how do you regard illness?"
Vicka: "The Gospa said: 'When God gives an illness, a cross, one must accept it with joy, with love, not to ask: Why has God sent me this cross rather someone else?' No, no! God knows why He has given it, and when He is going to free you from it. We only have to keep our hearts free in order to accept what He gives us."

Question: "The apparitions continue in your small room, but no longer at a fixed hour?"
Vicka: "The Gospa comes when she wants every day. It was this way when I was in the Holy Land." (where she went on a trip in 1987).

"Twice I was able to observe the coming of the apparition. After a very lively conversation, Vicka seemed to sense another presence. She began to collect her thoughts, and then, with a smile, she withdrew, she went off, she made us understand that we had to leave her alone."

Question: "Do you have the desire to become a religious?"
Vicka: "Let us see where the will of God is, what He wants.

It is no problem. Does He want me here? Does He want me in Heaven? It is all the same to me."

Question: "Do you have any worries about your future?"

Vicka: "No, none."

Question: "You have given your heart to the Gospa."

Vicka: "I have not given it to her, but I give it every day, step by step. To give everything to God: heart, soul and body. For me to give everything, and for God to take it. All want to free themselves from the cross, and they come to Medjugorje because of that. But they don't ask themselves why God gives this cross. God gives the cross because He wants to reach your heart. God looks for man's heart. It is here that the whole man is."

Question: "Why is it difficult?"

Vicka: "God wants to test your faith, to make you grow in faith. That alone is important: grow in the faith. Faith for us is like water for the flower. Without water, the flower dies. With water it grows. It becomes beautiful. The same with us. Without faith, we are as if we were dead. With a little faith, we have a little life. Little by little, faith can grow."

Question: "How do you regard the religious life?"

Vicka: "Beautiful, when all pray together, work, share their problems, mine and yours. In a community, there is equality. No one asks more than another. No, all are equal. Everyone says, 'We are brothers, we are sisters.' But words are only words. If I do not love and if I do not understand someone else's problem; if, for my brother, I am not ready to give my life to help him, to speak to him, or the sisters who forget to live for Jesus, who do not pray with the heart, are sad. They want to leave the convent, whether it may be after 15 years or 15 days. But how is it possible?"

Question: "And, Medjugorje?"

Vicka: "To believe in Medjugorje, or not to believe in it, is your free choice. The Gospa has not said, 'You must believe; you must not believe.' No. Do not worry about it. The Gospa does not make these distinctions. You are free. But when I pray with the heart, and I say, 'You are our

Mother, you are very near, open my heart,' then I feel that the Gospa comes very close to me, and then you are in Medjugorje."

Sister Margherita Makarovic relates that after the 23rd birthday of Vicka, (on September 3rd) and how, after a serious pneumonia of 20 days, which confined Vicka to bed during the end of August, she made herself tirelessly available (see Chronology).

Number 5

AN OPEN LETTER TO MONSIGNOR ZANIC

From Father Ivan Dugandzic
(Member of the First Two Commissions and
Spiritual Director of the Parish of Medjugorje)
September 22, 1987

Following Msgr. Zanic's sermon of July 25, 1987 (previously referred to) Friar Ivan Dugandzic, OFM (successor to Tomislav Vlasic and to Slavko Barbaric as Spiritual Director of Medjugorje), a member of the first two commissions of inquiry on Medjugorje (1982-1986), had been silent for nearly two months. But after the interdiction of the apparitions in the presbytery (September 9th), the meeting of Croatian bishops in Zagreb (September 16) and their letter of September 17th to the parish (previously mentioned) it seemed necessary to him to establish truth in clarifying some questions both basically, and of conscience, in the following letter:

Father Bishop,

Before long, two months will have passed since, in the presence of a shocked multitude of thousands of people, you evoked the "fire from hell," and you predicted for us, the priests of Medjugorje, a place "at the bottom" of the ladder. At the time, we had thought that you had allowed yourself to be carried through impulsiveness, but the last two months have refuted this interpretation. In fact, in your meetings with visitors, you do not cease to feed this fire, while for us, as a consolation, there only remains the certainty that it will not be you who will decide the place which each one of us must occupy in the beyond.

Recently, you have engaged in demonstrating that, here, it is Satan in person who is at work, and that since the time of Jesus Christ, it is the greatest deception (your words with Father Viktor Kosir).

What should one say to that? Would what Jesus held as impossible, that Satan be divided against himself, have become possible in our day? If that were the case "his kingdom would collapse." Or rather, perceiving that his old methods have not attained complete success, would he take refuge in prayer and in fasting? Father Bishop, you persist in not allowing any occasion to escape in order to slander or morally destroy every person bound to Medjugorje. You are hoping also of destroying Medjugorje itself.

This tactic most often invokes confusion and scandal to many souls. The American journalist, Jacqueline Srouji, who had spent months here in prayer, before returning to America, asked for an interview with Your Excellency. You received her on the 18th of September 1987. After two hours spent with you before the television camera and the microphone, she returned with tears in her eyes and told us:

"If someone had tried to persuade me that the Bishop hates you, I would have never believed him. After this interview, I know that he hates you."

[Author's note: I am in possession of the interview in question, but it has been communicated with the reference "reservatum," which I believe I have to respect.]

After your sermon on that Confirmation day at Medjugorje, and especially its publication in the press, many rubbed their hands with satisfaction, but many ask us why we keep silent.

After long reflection, I have decided to clarify some of your affirmations.

You state, "For six years I prayed, I studied, I remained silent." I think that you prayed although you often refuse the prayers which, at Medjugorje, are raised to God for you. I also think that you studied, but I know that you, like the commission, studied more the problematic introduced by you, than the phenomenon of the apparitions itself.

Your "silence" is a chapter on its own. If you would have kept silent, you would have demonstrated proof of prudence and wisdom. But, for a long time, you have always chosen to speak openly, and through that means to cast doubt in public opinion, accusing and judging not only the seers and the priests in Medjugorje, but also people who go there. All that culminated in the famous circular letter of October 30, 1984, which you had published for the whole world. It took the position that we, as a commission, had nothing else to do but to content ourselves in trying to show what you already knew beforehand.

In other respects, your vision on the role of the commission was confusing. You manipulated it according to what was agreeable to you. Once it was froth with consequences when you asked it to order and forbid something in your name. But when, on the contrary, someone suggested the possibility that this commission could arrive at a decision different from yours, in that case, the suggestion was not important and you knew how to say, "I am the commission."

The initiative undertaken by you, the day of Confirmation at Medjugorje, showed that you were persevering in the same behavior. You do not recognize the autonomy of the third commission, constituted by the Episcopal Conference of Yugoslavia, and you did not have the patience to wait for the results of its work. Previously, you would say that your responsibility was extremely great, but you were not willing to share it with the other bishops, as you had suggested for a long time. Now that the Congregation of the Faith has transferred the responsibilities to the Episcopal Conference, you do not accept this decision as having been given and in fact, you still persist in injecting your problems on "the phenomenon of Medjugorje."

Father Bishop, you asked us all, members of the former commission, for an oath to guard its secret. But you, first member of the commission, did not keep it. I cite only two instances:

—At the time of the inquiry, on the sealed envelope of Ivan Dragicevic [*Latest News,* No. 4, pgs. 17-23], the members of the commission were in agreement with him that the matter rest among us. But a few days later you spoke about it publicly to an important group of priests who had met at the Cathedral for a spiritual retreat.

—When the commission concluded its work in May '86, each one of us submitted to you, according to your wish, our written considered opinion. After that, you also asked that we vote, and that in secret. I asked immediately if the vote would remain truly secret, to which you responded with surprise, saying that this question was out of place. Then I reminded you of the violation of secrecy in the previously mentioned case, and that was not to your agreement. But perhaps, to give us the impression that this time the vote would really be secret, and would remain such, you did not communicate the result at all, even to us, members of the commission.

But you collected the data and dissolved the commission. Nevertheless, a few days later, many foreign priests returning from a discussion with you, propagated the negative results of the vote with figures which were not identical, but converged in that the great majority [of the commission dissolved] was against [the apparitions]. Our written responses and our vote are undoubtedly two different things, but [in both cases] you offered us only the two following possibilities:

a. constat de supernaturalitate: The supernatural has been established.
b. non constat de supernaturalitate: The supernatural has not been established.

The two psychiatrists maintained that the phenomenon needed further studies [in order to be able to conclude], and stated specifically that they, not being theologians, could not vote according to those terms. For this reason, they then abstained; and we, theologians (four among us), maintained likewise that the commission must continue its work, but we were in the minority and accepted the vote.

In the presentation of these votes, two things are disconcerting:

—You speak as though the 15 members had voted. At the time, only 13 took part in the vote.

—Still more disconcerting is the response to Question "b." You change it around into: Has it been established that it is not the supernatural? (Constat de non supernaturalitate). Now, the question provided for by the directives of the Congregation for the Doctrine of the Faith means: "In the current state of research, the hypothesis of the supernatural is not yet clear and remains open to further research." Your presentation of the results of the vote falsifies and distorts the information delivered to public opinion.

Father Bishop, you state that the events at Medjugorje have created tension and division in the Church: "Some believe in these apparitions and others do not."

How does one understand these words? Perhaps you want to say that before Medjugorje, in the Church of Hercegovina, there reigned unity and peace, and that all of that disappeared because some adhered to the apparitions and others did not. According to this logic, one should say also that at Lourdes and Fatima the apparitions divided the Church because there also, before approval by the Church, some went there on a pilgrimage and others remained indifferent. Up until now, a similar affirmation has not been maintained by anyone, since each one is free to go or not to go to these places. Here, the problem is different. Those who do not accept Medjugorje, do not accept even those who accept the apparitions, do not succeed in maintaining the serenity but become aggressive and ask that Medjugorje disappear.

You well recall, I am sure, the stormy meeting to which you convened us at the Episcopal Curia in November 1985. You then called the pastor, Father Tomislav Pervan, Father

Petar Ljubicic, me, Sister Janja Poras, and three seers: Marija Pavlovic, Ivan Dragicevic, and Jacov Colo. Before all of us, you pronounced this phrase of great weight:

> "Someone must disappear from Medjugorje, you,
> or I. I do not wish to disappear and I will utilize
> all the means at my disposal for that end."

And, really, since then, you have not made any discernment of the "means" or of the time and place where you would use them.

I must touch briefly on the case of the two friars of Mostar whom, often and willingly, you enjoyed involving in the question. Since the time when the preceding commission had been at work, many members, concerned in pleasing you, unceasingly threw out this question in our sessions. For this reason, in a session, I asked immediately that a subcommitte of three members be formed in the commission, with a responsibility of studying precisely this case and thus, of deleting it from the ledger of the day. You opposed it, and thus, this roadblock continued, subsequently to be brought up at each new session.

The general public did not know that these two young Franciscans had submitted their case to the Supreme Ecclesiastical Tribunal in Rome, the Apostolic Signature. The investigation showed some omissions and faults in the procedure by which they had been punished, and it was asked of them to choose an attorney. The process was initiated but was blocked, thanks to the powerful bond which you enjoy in Rome. Why do you fear the results? Are you convinced that everything has been done properly?

You spread everywhere through the world your lamentations on the existing division among the friars of Hercegovina, and correlatively on the friars of Medjugorje. But during all the time of your Episcopal mission in Mostar, you have done everything in Rome to make a normal life for this religious community impossible. The most recent example goes back only two months. Why did you create obstacles to make impossible the normal and democratic development of the mission of three visitors, who had been sent last May through our General Curia?[3] (See footnotes on page 131).

Father Bishop, every obedience in the Church has its roots in obedience to the faith which is common to us. Whoever is at the head of others should strive, through charity, to create the conditions so that one can obey in charity. But you can transform obedience into a dangerous weapon. You can create conditions where obedience becomes difficult or entirely impossible without betraying its own conscience and the interests of the Gospel.[4]

I would not know how to avoid stopping briefly on what you said in the Italian review "Jesus," on the subject of your sermon at Medjugorje (an article complementary of your sermon published in *"Famiglia Cristiana"*). What a hypocrisy in the explanation given by you of the worthy behavior of the parishoners confronting your provoking words. You state that the parishioners, by their silence, wanted to mean that they were henceforth tired of this story of the apparitions, and that they were in agreement with you. But what would you have said if they had reacted as the faithful at Mostar reacted in 1980 in the Franciscan church? You would have announced triumphantly to the whole world that the parish, of which one speaks as a place of peace, was in reality a rebel parish.

Here we are not successful in getting rid of evidence that you are looking for in order to provoke us. But in these six years, the parish has withstood many trials and has learned to serve peace beyond all that. Many testimonies from other parishes have told us how it has been painful for them to see the faithful of Medjugorje, their eyes moistened with tears, and they admired their worthy behavior. Besides, if you were so sure that the parishoners approved what you said, why, after Mass, didn't you exchange views with them as a good Father? But not even one word!

Father Bishop, this letter is not intended to be an attack nor an accusation, nor a calculation, but a self-defense. I have always believed in the ultimate victory of truth itself, even if it must come with due deliberation. In any case, public opinion perceives always more clearly who is the aggressor and who are the attacked in this matter.

Being then at the service of the message of peace, we cannot renounce love for truth, nor accept—against our personal conviction—a dictate of power. That would not be in the interest of the Church nor the Gospel.

In expressing to you the respect which I owe you, I remain in Jesus and Mary, your very devoted,

Friar Ivan Dugandzic

Number 6

CIRCULAR OF MONSIGNOR FRANIC, ARCHBISHOP OF SPLIT

President of the Doctrinal Commission of the Yugoslav Episcopat
On the Practical Conclusions Resulting from the Meeting Of Croatian Bishops on Medjugorje
September 16, 1987

The Council of Croatian Language of the Episcopal Conference [of Yugoslavia] met on September 16, 1987 in Zagreb for more than three hours, to discuss Medjugorje. From these discussions there emerged the following:

1. With respect to Medjugorje, one must distinguish clearly that:
   —The pilgrimages have become a world phenomenon because they come there, in increasing numbers from five continents, and,
   —Because of the alleged apparitions of the Madonna as well as her messages.
2. At this point one cannot ignore the numerous pilgrimages, nor abandon the faithful to themselves, but it is necessary for the priests to spiritually assist the pilgrims, and be at their disposal for confession, for preaching of the word of

God in their own language, and also for the celebration
of Holy Mass in their language.

3. With respect to scientific research conducted by specialists
of our country and from abroad, and particularly by the
new official commission, named by the Episcopal Conference of Yugoslavia, in obedience to a directive from the
Holy See on this question, we must be patient and give
such investigations full freedom.

The new commission is responsible to the Yugoslav Episcopal Conference, to arrive at a definitive opinion on the
supernatural character with the formula:

—The supernatural is evident-(constat de supernaturalitate),
or,

—(constat de non supernaturalitate)—It is evident that there
is no supernatural concerning said apparitions and
messages.

Up to that time, no bishop of the Yugoslav Episcopal
Conference can pronounce an appropriate official judgment
on these events, and it would have no official and con-
straining validity.

Only when the new commission has given its judgment
and it has been confirmed by the Yugoslav Episcopal Conference, and by the Holy See, then that judgment, be it
positive or negative, will have official merit which will bind
every Catholic in conscience.[5]

4. I repeat my interpretation according to which, the Yugoslav Episcopal Conference had, forbidden only "official"
pilgrimages, but not private pilgrimages or those organized
in a private manner.

5. In any case, I hold that one cannot affirm that these events
are believed through an act of faith, until the Church has pronounced its definitive judgment on the events of Medjugorje.
In the meantime, all of us who go to Medjugorje must go
there with a firm purpose of submitting ourselves to the definitive judgment of the Church. Meanwhile, we can have our
own opinions on these events, but not faith in such events.[6]

For this reason, it is not convenient for one to speak
of the messages of Medjugorje from the altar, nor is it

agreeable that these events be accused, in the name of God and in the Church, to be false or diabolical.

6. However, I hold that the faithful can go freely on a pilgrimage to Medjugorje, individually, or in pilgrimages which are privately organized. That is to say, in pilgrimages not organized by the Church as would be for example, a pilgrimage organized by the priest, the bishop, a convent, or by other similar ecclesiastical entities.

7. Priests can go on a pilgrimage to Medjugorje if they go there not as organizers of pilgrimages, but in the goal of assisting spiritually their own faithful, and with the firm intention of submitting themselves to the definitive judgment of the Church.

When someone asks them if they believe in the supernatural character of the events in Medjugorje, they can answer freely, but they should not believe in the events until the Church has officially pronounced on them.

8. It is not possible to believe even in the truths contained in Holy Scripture and in divine tradition, without the Church's guarantee that it deals with truths revealed by God.[7]

This attitude then is also applicable to private revelations. The difference lies in this, that the truths contained in public revelations[8] are binding in conscience for every Christian to accept them if he wants to be saved, where there exists no obligation for anyone (even after the definitive judgment of the Church over them) to accept private revelations since they are not necessary to salvation.

Only prudence can advise us to accept them when the Church declares that these apparitions are in harmony with public revelation. I prescribe that all of this serves as directives for my faithful, my priests and religious.

(Split, Sepember 23, 1987)

Archbishop

Frane Franic

(See footnotes on pages 131-132).

Number 7

INTERVIEW WITH JELENA

By P. Mannes, and the Pilgrims at Bolzano
November 22, 1987

Question: "Did the Gospa give you any signs with respect to your future?"

Jelena: "The Gospa didn't dictate any particular choice, but she told me: *You pray and the Lord will send you the light because prayer is our only light.* Then it is important to pray and that will make us understand the rest."

Question: "Then you are thinking. But finally, what did the Gospa say?"

Jelena: "The Gospa said to thank the Lord for everything that He gives us, and also to truly accept suffering and every cross with love, and to abandon ourselves to the Lord and also to be small before Him, because it is only when we abandon ourselves to Him that He is able to lead us on the authentically true and just way. When, on the contrary, we make lonely efforts, that leads us only to despair. It is necessary then to let Him do as He pleases. To be really very little before Him, always very little. Often the Lord also sends us suffering, so that we may become smaller before Him, to make us understand that by ourselves we are not able to do anything."

Question: "When a person dies, can they see us and help us?"

Jelena: "Of course, they can help us. That is why the Gospa says always to pray for the deceased, and our prayer will never be lost, even if he who is dear to us is in Heaven. Then the Madonna states: *If you pray for these souls, they will pray for you in Heaven.* It is necessary then to pray for them."

Question: "But is it true that they help us?"

Jelena: "Of course. We read it in The Creed, 'I believe in the communion of saints.'"

Question: "The Gospa asked for prayer, individual or community prayer?"

Jelena: "Yes. The Gospa insisted first of all on the importance of personal prayer. Then she added that Jesus asked us to pray together. So she wants to say that it is also important to pray together."

Question: "But how do we pray?"

Jelena: "Usually, when we are together, we recite the Rosary and general prayers, we read the Gospel and we meditate on it. But also, often, we try to abandon ourselves to spontaneous prayer."

Question: "Then, do you dialogue with Jesus?"

Jelena: "Usually it is He who speaks."

Question: "But is work also a prayer?"

Jelena: "Surely we must not abandon work. But in order to do it well, one must pray. When I prayed, even if everything goes very well, I succeed all the same in obtaining interior peace, otherwise I would lose it in the first instance. But, even in praying, if I begin to lose this peace, I have very much patience to begin again. Then the Gospa says, as I have understood her, *When you have not prayed and you have been so far from the Lord* (which occurs to me often), *then you do not succeed in understanding things well. You get lost in questions and thus all your life you think in doubt. But when, on the contrary, you truly pray, you receive a security and great force.* In speaking with others, with the neighbors, with friends, if we really do not pray, we are not able to speak nor to witness, nor to give an example of authentic Christian life. Now, we are truly responsible for all our brothers. The Gospa said, *Pray.* To me, for example, not too long ago she said, *Pray, pray, and prayer will lead you to the Light.* And really it was so. If one does not pray, he is not able to understand anything, and the words of others can only keep us at a distance. There is the danger. The Gospa also says: *If you pray, you will have assurance.*[9] Yes, the Gospa says: *It is important to do good for one's neighbor, but first of all, it is necessary to give all the importance to the Lord. Pray!*

"It is necessary to understand, but often we understand only by ourselves, and when one prays little, one has quite difficulty praying, and one does not succeed in even helping others. Really then, the devil tempts us. Only the Lord can help us do these things, and for that the Gospa tells us: *Do not worry, He will take you on the right path.*"

Question: "Did the Gospa ask you to pray at special times?"

Jelena: "Yes, she asked us to pray in the morning, in the evening, during the day, when one finds the time. She told us that we must set aside some time for it. But really, no matter how little that we do, it is with love that one must do it. And later, when one has more time, a rather free day, then give time to prayer, rather than to so many other things of lesser value.

Question: "Like today, Sunday, for example?"

Jelena: "Yes!"

Question: "The Gospa teaches you then, so that there is a possibility of knowing from her, if she wishes that a particular work be done; for example, for the sick or those who suffer, for the welcome of the youth? If one asks her, or if one is looking for a light on that, is there a response?"

Jelena: "For that, I have not asked of the Gospa. I only know one thing; that there are organizations, initiatives for good things, but very little prayer. Thus, one places more importance on doing, than on praying, and that is why the world changes so little. The Gospa says very simply that it is necessary to put yourselves before Jesus, and to help others. Very simple. But the Gospa has never indicated to us special means to help others. Help them as it has been given to you. Yes! The first who need our help are those who are close to us, our parents, our neighbors, whom we often help less than others. A girl told me that Mother Teresa told the young people: 'The family is the school of love, then it is there that one must begin.' The Gospa says likewise: *Pray also in the family.* (interview of November 22, 1987).

Number 8

A MEDAL OF OUR LADY OF MEDJUGORJE?

A FRAUD

Since autumn, 1986, I received dozens of letters, sending me (with indignation) an advertisement which had been promoted in many diverse periodicals, (religious, also on television), or sent to homes with enticing words.

Under a picture of Vicka, (identified for the occasion as "Ivanka") one found first of all a secret: "I met Ivanka and she confided her secret to me." It purported that this medal, on sale through this leaflet, was an infallible lucky charm. Included were some large blue titles with enticing explanations:

"A medal which has brought me happiness!"
"An extraordinary power!"
"I, who had never played, I bought a lottery ticket, and on the following day, I could hardly believe my eyes. I had just won [...]. My medal had brought me everything. And if I am happy today, I owe it to her, and to her alone."

Following, were pseudo-testimonies assuring the benefits of the medals: money, love, health. And the details on how to purchase, on page 4:

"It is not necessary that you be a practicing Catholic, or even a great believer in order to wear this medal and to benefit from its many powers, because the Blessed Virgin of Medjugorje protects, and brings happiness to all those who are really in need of it."

This theme was taken up with insistence in personalized letters:

Dear Sir or Madame X: (with the exact name repeated several times and with the signature, "Maria-Laure")
"I know well that you do not often go to church, but I also know that you have kept in the bottom of

your heart, a belief [. . .]. Mister X, when you wear your medal around your neck, the Virgin of Medjugorje will protect you, and will bring you what you really need: good health, love, fortune. Only one condition, Mister X, that you do not ever separate yourself from it, and that you always carry it on you [. . .]."

"You are among a few privileged individuals who have been selected to participate in the drawing of lots, which will be carried out by Mr. Pacella, officer of the court, etc. [. . .]. Do not hesitate any longer, Mister X. Remember that it is not absolutely necessary that you be a church-goer in order for you to carry this medal, and for it to bring you benefits, because the good Virgin of Medjugorje protects and brings fortune to all those who are really in need and who really confide in her."

I advised all those who expressed their indignation to me, to protest, and to act. I did so myself, because one of the pictures that had been reproduced, had been printed with the caption, "Laurentin Collection." This gave me the right to follow up. The publicity ceased during the middle of 1987. It seems to have continued only in a much smaller way. If it had continued, it would have been necessary to act legally, as I told all my correspondents, and the bishop where the "postal box" of the fraud was located, a French center of distribution.

It is superfulous to underline the errors, inventions, and grave omissions of these leaflets, which discredit Medjugorje in the eyes of all those who received this propaganda. In their eyes, this great movement of grace was transferred into a superstition of a low level, where Heaven has no other function except to obtain for us material goods, or illusions on this earth.

PUBLISHER'S FOOTNOTE

Similar material has been received by many in the United States, including the offering for sale of "special blessed stones" from the hill of apparitions, highly polished, (and highly priced). The publisher recommends total avoidance of all such promotions.

A PRIVATE INITIATIVE

From another source, I received, without publicity, a discreet Medjugorje medal, accurately reproduced. I questioned the man who had sent it to me. He answered me:

"It comes from the establishment, B. de Saumur, where one of my children works. It would have been made at the request of Belges, whose identity I did not know. I have sent it to you as information, but I do not participate in its distribution, since I do not have the soul of a merchant of medals (moreover, not asked by the Gospa). To my eyes, there must remain in circulation, only the miraculous medal of the rue du Bac; which I generously distribute to whomever wants it, at the end of my conferences on Medjugorje."

It is wisdom itself. If the editions and commentaries of the new Canon Law, which I have consulted, do not give reference to any regulation with respect to medals, one could say, that as long as an apparition is not recognized, the public dissemination of a specific medal would be premature. But, in this domain, as in others, the personal and private expression of piety remains a domain of freedom, left to the discretion and the prudence of Christians, the flip side of repression or indiscreet propaganda.

Number 9

INTERVIEW WITH MSGR. FRANIC BY A GROUP OF LAY PEOPLE FROM ANCONE

Split, December 22, 1987 (extract)

Msgr. Franic: "Is this your first visit to Medjugorje? For my part, I have gone there 12 or 13 times..."
Interviewer: "Our bishop is against it."

Msgr. Franic: "He is against it? It is all right. I am favorable to it. But this deals with free things, as St. Augustine says: 'in dubiis liberta in omnibus caritas.' I understand, then, the reasons of the bishops who are against it, but I would be happy if the bishops who are against it, understood the reasons of the bishops who are favorable to it. In any case, the Madonna teaches obedience. Has your bishop forbidden going to Medjugorje?"

Interviewer: "To us lay people, he cannot forbid."

Msgr. Franic: "If he does not forbid it, then go there. I allow my diocesan faithful, and I think that some Yugoslav bishops have expressed displeasure over these private pilgrimages. One goes there freely, even from the diocese of Mostar. . . .On December 17, to celebrate the 37th year of my episcopacy, I was there to celebrate Mass. I said it in the sacristy in private."

Question: "What do you think of the position taken by Msgr. Zanic in his sermon of July 25."

Msgr. Franic: "He can express a private opinion, just like I do when I say that I am favorable to it. I am convinced that the Madonna appears in Medjugorje, but it is my personal opinion, and one must wait for the definitive judgment of the Church. My personal opinion is worth as much as is the opinion of the Bishop of Mostar, or of the Bishop of Ancone. . ."

Question: "Excellency, has the Pope ever spoken to you about Medjugorje?

Msgr. Franic: "No, I do not want to create any problems for the Holy Father. Nevertheless, last July there was a pilgrimage of young people (there were almost 1,000). We said the Mass at Castelgandolfo, and, among the young people, I saw Mirjana from Sarajevo, where she is a student. I said spontaneously: 'Holy Father, here is a seer from Medjugorje!' The Pope answered: 'I pray each day for a good solution for Medjugorje.' There you see how he expressed himself, and I insisted: 'But, Holy Father, it would suffice for you to come to Medjugorje for a visit.' The Pope answered, 'It is not easy for the Pope.' 'But in private,' I said. And the Pope: 'The

Pope would not be able to go there, even in private.'

"I wanted to say, 'How come you have gone skiing to Gran Sasso?' but I stopped (here the bishop smiles). The Pope did not say any more, but I felt he had been interiorly open."

Question: "What can you say with respect to the opposition of the majority of priests regarding Medjugorje:"

Msgr. Franic: "Here also the majority of priests are against it, but the lay people are favorable to it. There is a crisis of prayer among us priests. It is necessary to recognize it. . .When evening comes, we sit ourselves before the television for three hours, without any problems, and say that we do not have the time for a small prayer group of fifty persons, and during that time, what does one do? One watches sports, football and other movies which we say are important, but we waste our time. . ."

Question: "I know that you must soon leave this diocese (having attained the age limit of 75 years, on December 29, 1987.) Many priests ask me to ask you where you will go because they will want to see you again."

Msgr. Franic: "I will stay here, if God wants." [He is a native of Split.] "But in leaving the entire place to my successor, if God wants I will stay here in a little apartment, and I will be at your disposal."

Question: "Will you still receive groups of pilgrims to guide them a little?"

Msgr. Zanic: "I will not do it if my successor forbids me. I hope not. I have a natural right, a personal right to freedom. But, who knows? I do not want to create problems for my successor."

Question: "How do you explain the relentlessness of the Bishop of Mostar against Medjugorje?"

Msgr. Zanic: "It is difficult to understand a soul. It is I who made him a canon. I recalled him from a distant parish to a parish in Split. I named him Pastor of the Cathedral. I am older than he. He is from 1918—six years difference. I knew him well, and many other priests did not know him. He is an intelligent man. The last sermon (at Medjugorje) was like a bomb which explodes in the whole world. Every day he says the Rosary and meditates. He is convinced. I cannot doubt his honesty."

Question: "In Italy, many priests laugh at us when we go to ask them for their blessing. When we speak to them of fasting, they say, 'The Gospel doesn't speak about that.' What do you think?"

Msgr. Franic: "The Church orders only two days of fasting: Ash Wednesday and Good Friday. But the Council recommends it. The Bible recommends fasting and prayer, with conversion. These are Biblical penances. The pharisees fasted twice a week. Jesus answered them, *"My disciples will fast when I will have been taken from them."* In the history of the Church, we find great penances. Then who can laugh at them? To condemn penance and fasting is to cast off the spirit of the Madonna, who asked very clearly, for fasting on bread and water on Friday and on Wednesday. In fact, among our people, it was already a tradition, and many women fasted during the entire Lenten period on bread and water."

NOTE: On visiting Ivanka on March 26, 1988, I learned that she had thus fasted all of Lent on bread and water. I did not learn about it from her, but from her circle of friends. When I spoke to her about it, she did not deny it, and I did not want to insist because she doesn't like this kind of questioning. It was on leaving her house that I asked myself, "But how did she nourish her child?" In fact, she weaned her a little before Lent, at the end of three months, according to the most frequent local practice...

For the same reason, I did not dare persist on the question which I asked her: "How does the mother of a family, who has been a seer, pray?"

"I am not really strong on prayer," she said to me. "I pray in the evening."

In fact, she attends Sunday Mass regularly, and, during Lent at least, each week she went to make a long prayer vigil with her husband, on the hill of Mt. Krizevac, at the foot of which she lives.

Number 10

THE MEETING BETWEEN PRESIDENT REAGAN AND GORBACHEV

Intercessory Prayer From Maria Pavlovic

Here are the circumstances which I have been able to gather: The American Ambassador, Alfred H. Kingon, had spent two weeks in Medjugorje in 1987. He had met Maria, and the idea came up that she should write a letter to President Reagan. Mr. Kingon promised to deliver it to him personally. Here is the translation of Maria's letter:

Dear President Reagan,

The Mother of God appears every day in this village of Medjugorje in Yugoslavia. She gives us a message of peace. We know that you are making efforts for peace in the world, and we pray each day for you. We want to let you know that you can count on our prayers and our sacrifices. We wish to help you, in this manner, in your heavy task. Our Holy Mother told us that one can avoid wars through prayer and fasting. I hope that this message will help you, and that the daily apparitions will be for you a sign that God loves His people.

United in prayer, in the Heart of Jesus and the Heart of Mary, we express to you our love and we greet you in peace, through the Queen of Peace.

Maria Pavlovic

The message was delivered to President Reagan before his meeting with Michael Gorbachev, at the beginning of December 1987.

On December 8, Ambassador A. H. Kingon telephoned from Brussels: "The President would have wanted to call Maria himself," he said, "but even at this moment, he is in conference with Michael Gorbachev. I have delivered the message to him, and he was very enthusiastic about it. After he had read it, he said, 'Now I am going to this meeting with Gorbachev with a new spirit.' "

This first call took place a little before 8:00 P.M. while Maria was still at Mass, and it was her friend Kathleen (the American) who took it. Later on that same evening of December 8th, the phone rang again at Maria's, and Kathleen thought that this time it was President Reagan himself who was calling from Washington. But the conversation was cut off at the beginning, and that happened again three more times. Each time the line was cut off.

Consequently, on December 14, Ambassador A. H. Kingon wrote a letter to Maria asking her to write a message of peace to the leader of the Soviet Party. He would make sure that the Ambassador of the United States in Moscow would transmit personally the message to Michael Gorbachev. He added:

"It would be wonderful for the two heads of state, of the two most powerful countries in the world, to be informed of your prayers and know the message of the Blessed Virgin."

Around Christmas, Maria received a photograph from Reagan with these words written in his hand:

To the seer, Maria Pavlovic, cordial greetings. I thank you and I wish you everything for the best. May God Bless you.

Sincerely,

Ronald Reagan

Number 11

American Attacks Against Medjugorje From the Right and From the Left

(A letter from Fr. René Laurentin to The Riehle Foundation)

Dear Bill Reck:

Following the recent controversies against Medjugorje, published in October 1988, you asked for permission to include, as part of the appendix of this present volume, pages 50 to 53 of my book, "La Prolongation des Apparitions de Medjugorje—1986," with possible additions.

I shall not add any additions, since these pages contain all that is important, and I decline adding anything for the morbid curiosity of the polemist. The latter, (who had no other goal than to attribute to a priest, close to Medjugorje, the birth of a child, aged 12 today) uses very aggressive police methods. He succeeded in finding a telephone number where I could be reached at a place where they protect my work. I began by answering him as a matter of courtesy, but I quickly perceived the defamatory and repugnant character of his undertaking, which showed little respect for either the truth or discernment, as well as little respect for the people concerned. It is for these reasons (and not out of embarrassment as he claims), that I refused to answer this very stubborn caller, who tried to prolong our conversation.

I repeated to him courteously that what I had to say, I had already said in my book, "La Prolongation des Apparitions de Medjugorje."

"I respect your freedom of interpretation, although I do not share it," I told him. "And I do not authorize you to take into account, this entrapment of a conversation." That, he did not fail to do by arranging it in his own way and intrepreting my non-answers as admission of what he had planned in advance.

The following telephone conversation, and its follow-ups, confirmed beyond all expression, what the priest, who had been unjustly accused, told me when I went to interview and invite him to defend himself.

"I will not defend myself. That would be to sink into degradation. The Blessed Virgin and the truth will suffice to defend me. I took care, and will continue to take care, not to sink any more deeply in this controversy, foreign to the facts of Medjugorje, as well as to the most elementary discretion. The precept: 'Nec nominetur in vobis' (*Eph.* 5:3), is applicable both to defamation as well as to fornication. It is vain to attach oneself to that which is unclean."

In 1986, when I wrote on this somber affair the pages that follow, it was to dispel the errors which had been insidiously disseminated. There, as elsewhere, I intervened out of responsibility, to assist a person in need, (in danger, as a matter of fact) in avoiding the controversy which degrades what it touches. The priest, who had been so slandered, has to his credit, more conversions and spiritual awakenings than 999 out of 1000 priests whom I know. When I asked Cardinal Urs Von Balthasar, who knew him well, what he thought of him, he answered me:

"That is how I imagine holiness."

This ardent and prophetic holiness makes this priest vulnerable. Others have since attacked his doctrine and his spirituality with an ill-will that only their zeal and their sincerity excuse. This priest has offered his life in union with the cross of Christ. His offering seems to have been accepted. He suffers from abandonment from his friends, and he has become the target of his enemies.

I abide by my text of 1986, which you have asked me to publish with the exact differences which I wrote on each point, according to its certainty or its probability. These pages rest on a confidential dossier which I was able to obtain, and on several confidential conversations at various levels. In this text, I voluntarily kept silent on the names of the persons who were accused, out of respect for the persons, and at the request demanded by interested parties.

What mental pathology can drive the adversaries of Medjugorje to go on and on about a fault which happened years ago and which has been worthily rectified? It concerns the personal and private life of two people. The mother of the child denies that the accused, on whom judgment is made (and by what right?), is the father of the child. She asks for discretion, to which she has the right. It is scandalous that the article, of October 1988, drags through the mud this harmless person, impugns her word, and speaks with scornful irony of the bad German accent of this person in exile. After she had worthily and discreetly remedied her error of long ago, she does not deserve to be the object of such Watergate-type tactics, by a press with few scruples, which claims to have the secret.

In protest against the slander concerning the paternity of the child, this mother left the security of a guaranteed position (and home for her and her child) with a kindly old man, and chose to return to a precarious situation. These calamities, then, cost her most dearly in a very difficult life. Since she is defenseless, her slanderer does not use any gloves to mistreat her. This dissemination is less legitimate than the affair of 1976 has with any relationship to Medjugorje, where the apparitions began in 1981. The only reason for anyone returning to this past event is that which makes flies rush to carrion and rotten flesh, and makes them forget the rest of the landscape.

It is for all of these reasons that I will not become involved in a vain and degrading controversy. To redress, or correct, so many assertions (or evil and free interpretations), one would never be able to end them, and one would only sink more in the degradation. This injurious, harmful climate is most regrettable. The part which I undertook to openly state the whole truth makes me fear, now, that the least phrase will be exploited in order to transform truth into slander or filth.

Apparently, there is currently an American plot against Medjugorje, and at a time when one has recorded more than 300 prayer groups, born from the message of the apparitions (and it seems there may be as many more). There is a real attack against this movement of prayer and of fast. It is a floodtide which tends to submerge so much corruption in the correspondence and designs of those who are plotting on a rather large scale. I have been able to read, from the pen of one of these protagonists, ("I will destroy Medjugorje, I will destroy Laurentin") whose acts, traps and disseminations have also begun against me, and I will not spend any time in defending myself. I will leave that to others, and I will continue my basic work and assistance to persons in need, in spite of the fact of the many blows to which this will expose me. I had never undergone so many calumnies, both varied and vain, prior to devoting myself to Medjugorje. I pray that the adversaries, whose slogan is "fidelity" (that is to say: faith, truth, respect for God and for mankind), put their slogan into practice. Let them renounce the Pharisaic temptation to justify their own faults in exposing and exaggerating those of others. Let them not continue to hurl a stone against the woman whom Christ has pardoned. The Pharisees themselves give them here a good example.

Since these men have zeal for justice and morality, instead of exhuming distant and obscure faults which belong to the past, let them devote their efforts to remedy the process which tends to multiply such faults, including the clergy. The opinion in vogue, that sexuality is a private affair and that any abnormality would be compatible with entrance into the seminary and the life of the priesthood, is propagating itself. Two years ago, there was published in NEWSWEEK, a document on this degradation of morals which did much harm to the Episcopalian Church, and progressed in the Catholic Church of the United States. No one, to my knowledge, has refuted the grave statistics that were furnished. And, one has not sufficiently tried to identify the causes of the evil and to remedy it. Yet, that is what is important for the future. It is not through defamatory articles, but through discreet, adaptable and deep actions that one will restore the seminaries that are corrupted on the model of those which are loyal . . .the majority of them.

Let the polemists learn to see the good which abounds instead of exhuming the sins of a distant past, of disguising them and of magnifying them under a microscope. Let them serve, also, the work of God, which is so marvelous at Medjugorje. That is why the diabolist (devil), whose name means divider, works desperately hard to destroy it. At Medjugorje, it is often necessary to have up to 150 confessors a day...thorough, overwhelming, lasting confessions, which remain God's secret. Let the people, slaves of their sins (including sexual), laity or clergy, return to normalcy through fasting and prayer. How many drug addicts, Don Juans, homosexuals, have radically changed their lives?

At the remarkable symposium at Leutesdorf (Msgr. Franic presiding) I was given the responsibility to discuss (for the remission of my sins) this annoying topic: "The Interecclesiastic Oppositions Which Medjugorje Suffers." I issued a document, which was both extensive and disheartening, where the extreme right and the lasting, social-culture left agreed to slander Medjugorje (and its protagonists) without ever having been there—with a few rare exceptions. This analysis led to one solid and comforting conclusion: reconciliations are making progress at Medjugorje, including those between the bishop (obedient to Rome, of whom I am happy to speak highly here) and the Franciscans. There remain only these irresponsible polemists, of the right and of the left, for whom one needs to pray, so that, in their turn, they may understand this work of grace (recognized by Msgr. Zanic himself), which daily multiplies conversions, prayer, fasting and unqualified sacrifices in the service of Christ and Our Lady.

It is in this spirit that one will be able to read the text of 1986, which publication I am authorizing in this book. At that time, this text had attained its goal of cutting short a slander, which spread all over Europe, and which became magnified and distorted. The deleterious climate created by the controversy made the publication of this original text timely, but which risked being attacked and misunderstood. It is with these expectations, and under these reservations, that I now authorize its reproduction, hoping that it will be read with a different spirit.

Sincerely,

René Laurentin

PUBLISHER'S FOOTNOTE

In Father Laurentin's book, "The Apparitions at Medjugorje Prolonged," published by The Riehle Foundation, the original French edition ("La Prolongation Des Apparitions de Medjugorje") included the following pages of text relative to the pregnancy issue. At the time of the French publication, this accusation was well-known throughout Europe, particulary France and Italy. It was little known in the United States and we chose not to include it in the English version in May 1987, at the time of printing.

AN ACCUSATION (1986 Text)

On November 28, 1985, the three priests of the parish (Ivan Dugandzic, Tomislav Pervan, and Pero) were called to the Bishops House at Mostar with three seers present: Maria, Ivan and young Jakov (then 14 years old), as well as Sister Jania, responsible for the community of sisters at Medjugorje (to date transferred as vice-provincial). The bishop announced to them what seemed to be, for him, great news: A Franciscan, formerly assigned to the parish, had fathered a child nine years previously with an ex-Franciscan nun, who had left then for a neighboring country. "The information has been sent to me from Rome by Cardinal 'X'", he related insistently.

"This matter is foreign to the apparitions at Medjugorje. It is five years prior to it. Why does that concern us?" wondered the astonished visitors.

As a matter of fact, they knew the instructions of the Congregation of the Faith, dated February 25, 1978, according to which, in matters of recognition of apparitions:

> "Gravely immoral acts cannot be held as negative signs which have been committed during or on the occasion of apparitions by those who are involved in them, nor those which were prior, later or external to the apparitions (Document of 1978, I, B, d)."

The declared accusation against the man could not have shocked them more.

During the preceding and following days, the bishop had spread the same accusation to several visitors (notably doctors who had come from Italy, and among others) who noted the triumphant tone of the accusation, as though this fact had constituted a decisive argument against the apparitions.

"It is necessary for me to die or for Medjugorje to die," retorted the bishop to those who were shocked at his vehemence.

The rumor, coming from so high, spread like wildfire over most of Europe. At Nice, France, it had taken the following strange twist when someone said to me, "It seems that one of the seers had had a child by a Franciscan."

The chronic misinformation about Medjugorje favored the most absurd errors. However miserable these pieces of gossip may be, the basic concern for truth invites us to dispel them.

The accusations spread secretly for a year in high circles. Msgr. Zanic had disseminated it in the Yugoslavian Episcopal Conference, then some confidants, from whom I have learned about it. Hardly knowing the accused, they did not know what to think at all, and presumed its validity because of confidence in their colleague. Others, knowing the accused, would moreover raise the question: "Is his current state that of an innocent person or of a penitent?"

It was in November 1985, after he had received a written denunciation from Mr. "O," that Msgr. Zanic openly made known the accusation. He presented it as having come with the authority of a Cardinal from Rome, who had only sent it on to him; in fact the old man (Mr. "O") seemed to intend it for the Bishop of the place only so that he might deal severely with the accused.

It is only on December 12, 1985, that Msgr. Zanic brings the accused into the presence of his provincial, to tell him, in substance,

> "Such is the accusation. If you admit that the Blessed Virgin is not appearing and that it is you who have staged all that, this matter can be taken care of."

The accused priest, on whom the bishop had already heaped derogatory labels (mentally sick, hoaxer, manipulator, etc.) answered,

"The Blessed Virgin is appearing; I cannot say
anything to the contrary. As regards the accusation,
why am I the last to be informed, and not the first?"

After November 26, those who had heard the accusation
had come to question the person who had been presumed
guilty. But he established as a principle, not to answer: "That
would be to sink into degradation. The Blessed Virgin and
truth will suffice to defend me," he answered in substance.
This noble attitude did not add any information, but the seers
had already confirmed this refusal to every form of defense.
"Let the Gospa defend you," they said to him.

Without giving any names, because the mother of the child
is also entitled to discretion, I will limit myself to the substance. I do it having in my possession a complete dossier
of the matter, which was patiently checked.

It is true that a Croatian Franciscan nun, whose presence
had been a problem in three successive convents, had a child
who was born January 25, 1977. She was relieved from her
vows. The presumed father of the child left the order and
went to America where he married, after being reduced to
the lay state. The Franciscans were humanely concerned in
obtaining honorable assistance for this woman. An elderly
widower in his eighties, who had lost his wife in 1976, took
her into his home in a neighboring country in all Christian
kindness. She came to his house as housekeeper, to maintain
his home. This upright man was most pleased with her service, and he maintained paternal relations with the child, who
called him Pappy.

It was on October 13, 1976, that a Franciscan had recommended this solution, at a time when this woman had no other
recourse than to leave for Australia. She initially refused this
life-saver, out of dignity and concern for bringing upon herself this impossible situation. Finding no other answer she
finally accepted 12 days later, on October 25 after 11:00 o'clock.

In November 1984, Bishop Zanic, accompanied by an inter-
preter, went to visit this old man, who had become blind.
The conversation stirred up the suspicions and scruples of

this man. He finally expressed them in a three page letter, dated from October 13-14, 1985, accompanied by a seven page typed report. These texts are rather ambiguous since the old man had dictated them because he was blind. He sent these two texts to Rome, along with other papers concerning the accusation: an undated letter which he attributed to the ex-nun, and three letters from the accused, who had kept a harmless correspondence with her (Christmas greetings on December 15, 1981, and an answer to Easter greetings in March 1981 and 1982), because he had been her superior at the time of the event. He had established a rule not to speak about her situation, undoubtedly because he had received at that time, some admission on the matter.

The mother of the child only learned about the denunciation afterwards through a rumor. On December 26, 1985, she addressed a firm written protest to the Bishop of Mostar. . . which follows:

> "The letter about me, which you have put in the dossier of accusation, is not mine, and those who have taken it into account, know well, because I had told you last Spring (1985):
>
> > 'Your Excellency, this letter is not mine; it is not my handwriting. . .I have told no one who the father of my child is. It is my own private affair, of which I wish no longer to speak, and do not want anyone else to speak about it.'
>
> "As far as the old man, whom I had served and respected for nine years, when I learned what he had written in such a false way, without my knowing, that troubled me, so I was not able to do anything but to leave him immediately, and to leave his house. All of this has been done without my knowing. The age of 95 years of this man excuses his behavior,. . .but how can one rely on it?"

May these precise details put to rest, the defamation and the confusion that perpetuates. After much hesitation, I am certain on this point. But people, in extreme confusion, never cease to question me about it, and silence seemed to confirm the admission of an unsolvable problem. The truth is the only way out of this proliferation of things that are said which are not true.

The next day, the day after he had made his accusations in front of the representatives of the parish, the Bishop of Mostar presented the same dossier to the Investigative Commission. They were very astonished and asked:

"Why this communication? Why are you bringing this up in conjunction with these apparitions,
and what is it that you expect us to judge?"

NOTE: Less than six months later, this Investigating Commission, founded by the Bishop of Mostar in March
1984, was dissolved without having finished its work.

FOOTNOTES

1. More exactly, a letter from the secretary of this Congregation to the secretary of the Episcopal Conference. One asks himself why this confidential letter, which was in no way a decision nor a decree, was published in the press, with its overestimation which the sermon of the Bishop endorses here.

2. The text of the scope of the documents which are cited have been specifically stated in "Latest News No. 6."

3. It relates to the visit to the Province of Mostar by three persons sent from the Curie Generalice in Rome. They visited all the houses and voted for the election of the provincial in order to establish normal relations (the former Provincial who had been elected had been sent into exile where he died, and a successor was named in an authoritarian manner). A friar from Zagreb (Jozo Vasilj) was elected by 110 votes to 140. But this election remained in suspense until the date of this writing (Spring 1988).

4. A letter of March 25, 1985 ("Apparitions at Medjugorje Prolonged," pgs, 38-39) and the successive elimination of T. Vlasic, S. Barbaric, as spiritual directors at Medjugorje.

5. In order to avoid all ambiguity on this complex and discussed question, let us be precise. According to the norms of the Church, the official judgments of the Church on the authenticity of an apparition, in contrast to dogmatic judgments of faith, are conjectural interpretations by which the Church does not intend to bind consciences, as Monsignor Franic reminds us, but to guarantee only that there are good and serious reasons to believe in these apparitions which the Church advises one to believe or encourages belief in. A negative judgment has the same characteristic. Yet it can assume a more imperative and more absolute character if the authority of the Church identifies the characteristic errors concerning faith or morals.

6. Even here, theological doctrine is subtle and controversial. According to Karl Rahner, Congar, and others, those who believe in the apparitions in a private manner could have been gratified by God with a personal certainty of faith. Evidently, that does not give them a magisterium, but it deals with Divine faith since this faith results from a movement of God.

   On the other hand, many theologians believe that there, where the Church officially recognizes the apparitions, they believe that She authorizes or encourages not from Divine faith, but only human. Others have looked for other labels such as "ecclesiastic" to recover this domain which is difficult to appreciate. The distinctions which are confirmed here are many, notably between act of faith and act of the magisterium which pronounces a judgment on these facts, so difficult to discern and to evaluate.

7. Note of Monsignor Franic himself: (Cf. Saint Augustin, Contrar epistolam fundamenti, c. 5, No. 6, PL 42, 176): "Ego. . .Evangelio non crederem nisi me catholicae ecclesiae commoveret autoritas" (I would not believe in the Gospel if the authority of the Catholic Church would not lead me to it).

8. Documentation which opposes public revelation (the official revelation from God and from Christ stated in the Bible) to private revelations is today contested, because public revelation is revelation par excellence, but the revelations of Lourdes and Fatima have also had a public character. They have been addressed to the Church and to the Popes who have considered them, in making and ordering the whole Church to make the consecration requested at Fatima, for example. That is why one prefers today to distinguish between founding revelation and private revelations which do not have the same fundamental and universal scope.

9. Jelena finds again here, this assurance of which the New Testament is witness, and speaks so well—the certainty and boldness of the first Christians, in the service of Christ.

CHRONOLOGY

We summarize here the events of the 7th year of apparitions at Medjugorje, including those that have been reported in the different chapters.

1987

June 23: Beginning of my 15th trip to Medjugorje.

June 24: Arrival of crowds in Medjugorje. Toward 11:00 at night, apparition and special message to Maria on the hill of Krizevac (Chapter 1).

June 25: 150 confessors are needed for a crowd of 100,000 people. The calmness, the silence and the prayer exceeded everything which one had witnessed up to them.

From 6:44 P.M. to 6:55 P.M., Ivanka, who had come to her brother-in-law's house, has the second annual apparition which had been promised her for this anniversary of the first apparition. She then makes this brief communication: "The Virgin spoke to me particularly about the 1st and the 2nd secrets, and asked me to pray very much for that."

July 3: Father Gobbi receives, at Saint-Marin, an eschatological message converging with Mirjana's conviction: the apparitions of Mary were preparing for a return of Christ. But the eschatological error of the first Christians, and of the apostle Paul himself, through an optical illusion which brings long terms nearer, invites us to complete prudence on such prophecies. It seemed to announce the unveiling and realization of the secrets for 1987. And they remain in suspense.

July 23: Audience of John Paul II at Castelgandolfo, to a group of more than 1,000 young people, among whom was the seer Mirjana. Msgr. Franic introduced her to the Pope who said: "I pray each day for a good solution concerning Medjugorje."

The staff of the Pope, which stands watch and administers to his needs prevents the distribution of a picture, taken at this time, to avoid propaganda or inconsiderate rumors.

July 25: Msgr. Zanic celebrates Confirmation, on the feast of the patron saint of the parish, St. James, at Medjugorje.

His sermon against the apparitions claims "the fires of Hell" for those who support them. The shock is rude, but the parishioners, devoted to respect and obedience through fasting and prayer, listen in a respectful silence.

Rita Klaus, mother of an American family, having acquired multiple sclerosis since the 1960's, was cured on June 18, 1986, while praying to Our Lady of Medjugorje, wants to include her cure at the parish.

A young girl, a photo-model and high class prostitute in the environment of multi-millionaires, has just attained a rapid and profound conversion at Medjugorje through fasting and prayer. Her anonymous account, from September 24, 1987, has been translated above, (see chapter 6).

August 5: Anniversary of the birth of Mary, according to the seers, (who celebrated her 2,000 birthday on August 5, 1984). The tremendous crowd was estimated at nearly 100,000 persons, of whom there were 2,000 Hungarians. One also observed the presence of Chinese and of Africans.

August 15: Jakov, vacationing in Austria, returns to Medjugorje.

September 2: "Famiglia Cristiana" (Christian Family), the largest Italian weekly, published in its entirety, the indictment from Msgr. Zanic against Medjugorje (sermon of the preceding July 25). The news spread in the Italian and world press where the news became: "The bishop responsible for Medjugorje has condemned the apparitions and forbidden pilgrimages."

September 9: The bishop forbids the apparitions to take place, henceforth, in the rectory. There is great difficulty in finding a solution. The seers will have them in their homes, or without witnesses in the locked choir loft of the church.

September 13: Maria, in search of a solution, stays at home for the apparition, but in detriment to her attending daily Mass.

September 14: She takes refuge in the choir loft of the church (locked and without witnesses). This solution, supported by Fr. Maria of "Radio Maria," tends to prevail in the future.

A crowd for the Feast of the Holy Cross. Day and night prayer on the hill of Krizevac.

The "Compas" agency from Lubljana undertakes the construction of a hotel with 100 beds, 400 meters from the church of Medjugorje.

September 16: Assembly of the Croatian bishops in Zagreb to examine the situation created by Msgr. Zanic's sermon and its international publication. His colleagues reproach him for not having obeyed the directives of the Holy See, which removed him from judgment and which confided the new investigation, in progress, to the Episcopal Conference. They refused to have the bishop's sermon printed in the "official" journal of the Catholic Church, "Glaz Koncila."

They granted him new restrictions on the dissemination of the messages and the definition of "official pilgrimages," which included those which, not only the bishops, but the priests organized.

A little later, a note from Msgr. Franic, president of the "Doctrinal and Liturgical Commission" of the Episcopal Conference, will state precisely that the priests can and must normally accompany the pilgrimages, organized by lay people, in view of Masses, sermons, councils, confessions and spiritual direction needed.

September 22: An open letter from Fr. Ivan Dugandzic, former member of the Episcopal Commission, and spiritual director of Medjugorje, to Msgr. Zanic in deferential response to the sermon where they were vowed to "the fire of Hell." (see page 100).

October 23: During my 16th trip to Medjugorje, some representatives of the municipal government come to have lunch at the rectory, in order to discuss the designs for town planning of the pilgrimages, and to grant the parish the sale of the land of its old school (formerly confiscated and burned). They grant permission to build there, a necessary center for the pilgrimages.

October 28-30: A report of the (athiest) Crotian journalist, Miljenko Smoje in "Slobodna Dalmacija" (Free Dalmatia). The priests in Medjugorje communicated to him the statistic: "650,000 Communions distributed during the first nine months of 1987."

November 11: Ivanka brings her first daughter into the world—Christina. The birth took place rapidly and without problems, hardly an hour.

November 15: Fr. Tomislav Vlasic, who had spent a year in Italy, to a place that was not revealed, returned to Medjugorje and takes up contact with prayer groups. The members of one of them were involved in not making any decision concerning their life for four years. The time of decision had come and it is without doubt, one of the reasons for the visit of Fr. Tomislav. He was received with joy by many: "My legs could not hold me up because of my joy," said Maria. She thus evaluated the results of fasting by Fr. Tomislav: "Very lean, but great."

November 22: A word from Fr. Tomislav Vlasic to some pilgrims at the end of their brief stay in Medjugorje:

"I made a retreat of prayer, and I return in prayer because I understood that such is the urgency for the world and for God. Not only do we have a need for God's love, but God also has need for our love. That is the reason for my retreat and I offer my life in reparation for the sins of the world. May it not be but prayer and adoration."

His conclusion, "Pray! Pray! Pray! Because such was and such will be the last message of the Gospa."

December 8: Feast of the Immaculate Conception. Maria, who had written to President Reagan on the advice of her host and American friend Kathleen, to tell him of her prayer for peace, receives (a little before 8:00) from Ambassador Alfred Kingon, residing in Brussels, a telephone call on behalf of President Reagan inviting her to prayer for the signature of the accords in progress that evening in Washington. Another call coming from Washington and from the President himself, according to Kathleen, was interrupted three times (see note insert page 120).

December 17: Visit of Msgr. Franic to Medjugorje.

December 19-20: The seers, Maria, Ivan, Vicka, and it seems Mirjana, are called to Split where the doctors of the Episcopal Commission, notably Dr. Korljan, examined them.

December 20: Christina, Ivanka and Rajko Eliz's daughter,

must be Baptized today, a year less a few days after their marriage, but Rajko, denounced for some remarks which one called anti-government (anti-Serbian), had been sent to prison in mid-December. He was freed on December 28th. He has the habit: a cross which he wore as habit when he had begun his studies as a veterinarian, prevented him from being able to successfully complete them. The Baptism was delayed until January 10th.

December 28: About 10:00 P.M., the apparition for Maria and Ivan, on the hill of Podbrdo. The Blessed Virgin appeared with some angels, said Ivan. She blessed twice, the objects of the persons present, the second time, as she withdrew in the sign of a luminous cross.

1988

January 1: Some wished to make the way of the cross at Krizevac, in the evening after Mass. But the seers of the prayer groups made it known that the Blessed Virgin had asked them to remain in the homes for their vigil of prayer, for the first day of the year.

January 9: The Gospa asked Vicka for a new interruption of the apparitions, the fourth, which will last 50 days until February 29th. Vicka accepts this sacrifice without hesitation; she gave a warm welcome during those days and came regularly to Mass.

January 10: Maria becomes ill (the flu with fever), which, along with Vicka's interruption, cancels the trip to France for scientific and medical examinations. These tests had been prepared with the greatest discretion, but they were pointed out by "Eco."

January: Interview with Cardinal Tomasek: "The Iron Cardinal," in "Sveta Pastina," of January 1, 1988. He expresses his acknowledgment of the apparitions of Medjugorje: "Some important events. We have received very much from Mary through Medjugorje." (translation in "Eco").

February 26: Fr. Tomislav Vlasic returns to Medjugorje to lead to his retreat in Italy (somewhere in the Apennins), 12 girls and 3 boys from prayer groups, among whom were the seer Maria, her friend and American hostess Kathleen, and Maria Dugandzic. Also Agnes Heupel, a German cured at Medjugorje, and young Ignace, from Vienne. It was through a "desert" of five months where they lived in prayer and consecration, from the beginning of March until the end of July.

February 28: Maria and other members of the prayer group are at Terlizzi, near Bari, at Casa Betania of the Capucins, where the very long ecstasy of Maria, in the presence of some witnesses, was filmed on video, with authorization from the superior of this convent.

February 29: Vicka sees again, at the end of her fourth interruption of the apparitions, at the end of 50 days.

March 18: The sixth annual apparition to Mirjana in Sarajevo.

March 24: Important medical meeting of ARPA in Milan, on the perfect mental health of the seers of Medjugorje. (17-24 hours).

March 25: Tomislav Vlasic signs the document where he announces the establishment of his contemplative community. The importance given the messages of Agnes Heupel and the comparisons of their spiritual union with that of Francis of Assisi and St. Catherine of Siena will cause some criticism.

March 25-27: My 17th trip to Medjugorje.

April 12: The new meeting of bishops, under the presidency of Cardinal Kuharic, on the pastoral of Medjugorje.

April 27: Visit by Tomislav Vlasic, Maria Pavlovic (who has the apparition in the church), and Agnes Heupel at Priabona. (reported in "Eco" 53).

Start of May: Publication of the book "The Hidden Face of Medjugorje" (Saint Francois du Lac, Quebec, Editions Psilog), first volume of the book by Louis Belanger against Medjugorje. Fr. Rupcic very quickly wrote a criticism about it entitled "A Great Falsification."

May 28: Favorable account of the book by Sivric in "La Croix," by J. Potin. "These apparitions at Medjugorje are only a game for children, doing an imitation of Lourdes." Hundreds of letters of protest arrive at "La Croix" during the following days.

June 25: The 7th anniversary of the first apparitions on the hill of Podbrdo (and my 18th trip to Medjugorje). The third annual apparition to Ivanka.

June 30: "La Croix" faithfully publishes a page of testimonies, all favorable to the authenticity of Medjugorje.

July 7: Article by René Laurentin in "La Croix," focusing on this entire matter.

July 11: Maria (who left Tomislav's community on July 5th) disavows her testimony of April 21, published as an appendix to the letter of Tomislav Vlasic, dated March 25: The Blessed Virgin did not communicate to her any approval of the new community. Having been led away by her friends (adversaries of Tomisalv Vlasic) to Venice, Rome and Milan, Maria tries to do her best during the 40 days of retreat which the Blessed Virgin asked of her.

End of July: Anticipated pilgrimage of Tomislav Vlasic's community to Medjugorje in search of peaceful solutions.

August 14: Maria's return to Medjugorje, toward noon.

August 22: A new visit by the community of Tomislav Vlasic to Medjugorje. Maria Dugandzic and two other members will stay in Medjugorje while maintaining their spiritual bonds with the community. Tomislav is waiting to take a second group of 14.

September 9: This Friday, Msgr. Frane Franic, who had submitted his resignation because of age (75 years on December 9, 1987) receives the nomination of his successor: the parish priest of Markaska, one of his priests. The nomination became effective the following Sunday.

September 11: Celebration of the Feast of the Holy Cross. Enormous crowds on the Hill of Krizevac in the order of 200,000 persons.

September 25: End of the sufferings of Vicka, which she endured for several years. She was frequently siezed by a condition of severe lethargy, which her family called "her coma." When she felt this condition coming upon her, she would discreetly take refuge in her room. I saw here there, flopped in her bed, completely relaxed, but she was conscious. She suffered, and sometimes in this condition she had the apparitions. In

January 1988, the Blessed Virgin let her know that her trials would end on September 25th. On February 4th, Vicka told of it, confidentially and in writing, to her confidant, Father Bubalo. In February, she told it to two members of the commission, but she was not authorized to confide the date to them. She decided to submit it in writing in a sealed envelope, and she informed them ahead of time. She informed them four days before the end of her trial, on September 21st, and Msgr. Comarica, President of the Commission, came to verify it. It was his first trip to Medjugorje.

October 6: Arrival in Medjugorje of Father Leonard Orec, O.F.M., named pastor, as a replacement for Father Pervan, promoted to Counselor of the Province and Director of Studies.

Father Ivan Dugandzic is named Secretary of the new Provincial. Two other Franciscans are named to Medjugorje: Ivan Landeka (recognizable for his height and his moustache) and Victor Kosir. Fr. Slavko is named Vice-Master of Novices at Humat. This assignment brings him close to Medjugorje, and will permit him more freedom to continue his irreplaceable task of vigilant information and spiritual action there. Two members of the old team remain in the parish: Fathers Dobroslav Stojic and Pero Ljubicic, he who Mirjana has entrusted to reveal the secrets.

October 6-9: My 19th trip to Medjugorje.

October 17-20: A symposium on Medjugorje organized for the priests by Father Orec, in Leutesdorf (Germany), with Msgr. F. Franic, Slavko Barbaric, Dr. Korljan, K. Notslzinger (Vienne), M. Schroter (Heidelberg), Van Raab, R. Laurentin.

Fr. Slavko and the seers, Jakov and Ivan

Ivan during an apparition

Fr. Philip Pavich

Vicka meeting with the pilgrims

144

Fr. Slavko Barbaric

Fr. Slavko with Ivan during an apparition

The government supported souvenir stands

147

MEDJUGORJE
BY FATHER RENÉ LAURENTIN

The following works of Father Laurentin have been translated into English, and are currently available.

Is The Virgin Mary Appearing at Medjugorje?
By Word Among Us Press

The first book of the author on Medjugorje and a complete unfolding of the events through 1984.

Scientific and Medical Studies
By Veritas Co., Dublin, Ireland

Two years of the complete studies on the seers.

The Apparitions at Medjugorje Prolonged
By The Riehle Foundation

Update book through June, 1986.

Latest News—Sixth Anniversary
By The Riehle Foundation

Update book through June, 1987.

Messages and Teachings of Mary at Medjugorje
By The Riehle Foundation

700 messages and the application of the theology involved to Scripture and to Catholic Doctrine. Includes extensive study of the teachings of Mary at Medjugorje.

Learning From Medjugorje
By Word Among Us Press

An overview of the most important elements and how to incorporate this knowledge in our lives.

Seven Years of Apparitions
By The Riehle Foundation

Update book current through Fall, 1988.

THE RIEHLE FOUNDATION

The Riehle Foundation is a tax-exempt non-profit foundation distributing Catholic literature around the world. Since 1977, thousands of books, Bibles, rosaries, etc., have been sent free to missions and seminaries in third world countries, to hospitals, prison chaplains, etc.

The foundation is deeply committed to making known Our Lord's message of love and peace. Today it seems that message is being delivered to the world through Our Mother, Mary, at Medjugorje; a continuation of the Fatima message delivered in 1917.

The Riehle Foundation publishes several books on Medjugorje.

The Apparitions at Medjugorje Prolonged
By Fr. René Laurentin ($5)

Latest News of Medjugorje—June 1987
By Fr. René Laurentin ($4)

Our Lady of Medjugorje
With full color photos.
By Judith M. Albright ($3.50)

Our Lady Teaches About Prayer at Medjugorje
By Fr. Albert J. M. Shamon ($1)

The Gold Book of Prayers
By The Riehle Foundation ($2)

Messages and Teachings of Mary at Medjugorje
By The Riehle Foundation
700 messages and the application of the theology involved to Scripture and to Catholic Doctrine. Includes extensive study of the teachings of Mary at Medjugorje. ($7)

Copies may be ordered from THE RIEHLE FOUNDATION. Donations, though not required, are deeply appreciated. Suggested values for the above books are indicated.

Please write to:

THE RIEHLE FOUNDATION
P. O. Box 7
Milford, OH 45150

All contributions are used for the publishing and/or distribution costs of providing spiritual material to a world desperately in need of learning more about and living in God's peace and love.

In Tribute

Cardinal-designate Hans Urs von Balthasar died suddenly, on June 26, 1988, at age 82. It was just two days before he was to receive the red hat from Pope John Paul II.

Von Balthasar was considered by most as one of the foremost theologians of our times, and held in the highest esteem by authorities in the Church, including Pope John Paul, Cardinal du Lubac, Cardinal Ratzinger, and Karl Rahner, among others.

Von Balthasar spoke openly and often of Medjugorje, convinced of its authenticity. He stated that Medjugorje's beauty is, above all, in the glorified humanity and maternal love of Mary; the perfume of her holiness is everywhere. He felt that her presence is that which permeates Medjugorje with "God's better beauty—His grace."

Fr. Von Balthasar, stalwart leader and defender of the Church and Her teaching, found the same orthodoxy in Medjugorje. Concerning it, he stated:

> "Medjugorje's theology rings true. I am Convinced of it's truth. And everything about Medjugorje is authentic, in a Catholic sense. What's happening there is so evident, so convincing."

We join another of his friends, Fr. René Laurentin, in paying tribute to this special "son of Mary."

THE RIEHLE FOUNDATION